Tick...Tick...

Hear that clock ticking? It's the countdown to the AP English Language and Composition Exam, and it'll be here before you know it. Whether you have one year or one day to go, now's the time to start maximizing your score.

The Test Is Just a Few Months Away!

The rest of us are jealous—you're ahead of the game. But you still need to make the most of your time. Start on page 101, where we'll help you devise **year-round strategies** to make the most of your time so you'll be well-prepared for the big day.

Actually, I Only Have a Few Weeks!

Using our program, you still have time for a full review. Turn to **The Main Course**, where you'll find a **comprehensive guide** to the multiple-choice section and the essays, as well as a review of all the **rhetoric** you'll need to know.

Let's Be Honest. The Test Is Tomorrow and I'm Freaking Out!

No problem. Read through the **Brief Guides** to cracking each section (page 5). Then grab a pencil and take a **practice test** (page 111). Don't worry about the scores—just spend as much time as you can familiarizing yourself with how the test looks and what they want you to do. Before you go to bed, go through the **Checklist for the Night Before** (page 2) and keep it close. It'll walk you through the day ahead.

Relax. Everything you need to know, you've already learned. We're just here to keep it fresh in your mind for test day.

My Max Score

AP ENGLISH LANGUAGE AND COMPOSITION

Maximize Your Score in Less Time

Jocelyn Sisson

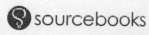 sourcebooks

Published by Sourcebooks, Inc.
P.O. Box 4410, Naperville, Illinois 60567-4410
(630) 961-3900
Fax: (630) 961-2168
www.sourcebooks.com

Library of Congress Cataloging-in-Publication Data

Sisson, Jocelyn.
  My max score AP English language and composition : maximize your score in less time
/ by Jocelyn Sisson.
       p. cm.
  1. Advanced placement programs (Education) 2. English language--Examinations--
Study guides. 3. Universities and colleges--Entrance examinations--Study guides. I.
Title.
  LB2353.62.S57 2010
  428.0076--dc22
                                    2010039350

Printed and bound in the United States of America.
                 VP 10 9 8 7 6 5 4 3 2 1

Contents

Acknowledgments

This book would not have been possible without the encouragement and mentorship of my friend and colleague Tony Armstrong. Tony taught me the value of the multiple-choice test and convinced me that I had a book to write. I also want to thank my friend and colleague Ed Coleman, whose help, both verbal and written, was greatly appreciated and extremely useful. No acknowledgment could be complete without thanking my husband, partner, and best friend David Craig. His support was unwavering, his advice invaluable, and his frustration level almost nonexistent. Finally I want to thank all of the students I have taught over the years. Without their responses and questions, I would not be the teacher I am today.

—Jocelyn Sisson

Introduction

Everybody comes to an AP test from a different place. For some, it's the one AP test of their high school career, while for others, it's just one of many. Some students have been focused on it all year, supplementing their classwork with extra practice at home. Other students haven't been able to devote the time they would like—perhaps other classes, extracurricular activities, after-school jobs, or other obligations have gotten in the way. Wherever you're coming from, this book can help. It's divided into three sections: a last-minute study guide to use the week before, a comprehensive review for those with more than a week to prepare, and a long-term study plan for students preparing well in advance.

Think of these sections as a suggestion rather than a rigid prescription. Feel free to pick and choose the pieces from each section that you find most helpful. If you have time, you should review everything—and, of course, take as many practice tests as you can.

Whether you have a day or a year to study, there are a few things you should know before diving in. For starters, what is the AP English Language and Composition Exam?

About the Exam

The AP English Language and Composition Exam lasts for three hours and fifteen minutes and consists of two sections, a multiple-choice section, and an essay section. The exam tests your ability both to read and write critically and accurately.

Section I contains four or five passages with fifty to fifty-five multiple-choice questions. This part of the exam tests your ability to read critically and answer questions accurately. More specifically, it requires you to recognize how authors use language and for what purpose. You have one hour to answer the multiple-choice questions.

Section II asks you to write three essays in three different modes: synthesis, analysis, and persuasion. You have two hours and fifteen minutes to plan and compose the essays. Although there are many similarities among the three essays, what the prompts demand and how you support your positions will differ.

The synthesis essay requires that you take a position on a subject and support it using evidence from the six to seven sources that the exam provides. In the rhetorical essay you are asked to identify and analyze the rhetorical strategies used by the author in a given passage. Finally, the persuasive essay requires you to take a position on a controversial issue or idea. Unlike the other two essays, however, no sources are provided, so you must use your own knowledge and experience to support your argument.

Scoring

The multiple-choice section is worth 45 percent of your score. Until recently, you were penalized one quarter of a point for each incorrect answer. This is no longer the case. Because no penalty points are incurred for incorrect answers, it is in your best interest to answer every question.

The essay section is worth 55 percent of your score. Each essay is scored on a scale of 1–9. (Refer to the scoring guide on page 77 to understand more specifically which type of essay earns which score.) The essays are always read by at least two readers, who are typically educators from around the country. The readers do not expect the essays to be polished masterpieces. They assess the essays by standards that are appropriate for rough drafts. Readers grade the essays holistically, meaning that the essays are judged as a whole, not by their individual parts, so there is no strict formula to grading the essays.

The scores from the three essays are added and combined with the multiple-choice score to generate a composite score, which is converted into a score of 1 to 5. The scale translates in the following way:

5   Extremely well qualified
4   Well qualified
3   Qualified
2   Possibly qualified
1   Not recommended for AP credit

Each college and university has its own guidelines for recognizing AP exams. Typically, if you earn a score of 5, and often a 4, the college or university of your choice will award you college credit, which may save you money or allow you to take another interesting class.

The Bad News

The class that prepares students for the AP Language and Composition Exam is a full-year class. It is a skills-based class, which means that practice is necessary to do well on the exam. It is very difficult to cram because, as with playing a musical instrument, practice makes perfect. You can't become a virtuoso by cramming. You can't do as well on the exam studying this book the night before the exam as you could do if you allowed yourself time to practice.

The Good News

The good news is that if you read and write regularly (a safe bet), you've been practicing all along. The more confident a writer you are, the higher you are likely to score on the exam. Of course, the AP Language and Composition Exam does test a specific type of reading and writing, and that's where this book comes in handy. By following the steps in this book, you can hone your writing to maximum effect in the exam. Learn the ins and outs of the test, review the rhetorical strategies, and, most importantly, take a practice test or two, and you should be prepared to do well on the exam.

Visit mymaxscore.com for an additional practice test for the AP English Language and Composition Exam, as well as practice tests for other AP subjects.

THE ESSENTIALS: A LAST-MINUTE STUDY GUIDE

Okay, so you've purchased this book a few nights before the exam, or maybe you've been preparing for weeks but still feel the need to cram at the last minute. With so little time remaining, is it time to panic? No, it's time to prepare. If you've been taking an AP English class, or preparing in other ways throughout the year, then you're nearly there. All you need now is to settle your nerves, review a few strategies to refresh your mind, and line everything up for test day. It's not too late to maximize your score.

Get focused. You don't have much time, so you'll want to make the most of the time you have. Turn off all your electronics and technological gadgetry. No texting or Web-surfing. Ask your family not to bother you unless it's really important. Close the door. Ready? Then let's get started.

Review the Test-Taking Tips

Start by reviewing "A Brief Guide to the Multiple Choice Section" on page 5. To help you know what you're in for in the essay section of the test, review the tips for approaching the essays beginning on page 9. There are different ways of dealing with each of the essay types, so be sure you're familiar with all three! If you have a little more time, go over the full sections on the Multiple Choice and Essay sections beginning on page 27.

Take a Practice Exam

This is the key to your last evening of preparation. Do the practice exam on page 111 in real time. Don't take a break or look at any of the answers until you've completed the entire exam. Use the practice test as a chance to practice your skills and identify any weaknesses. If you still have time, make the most of it by reviewing the areas that you need the most work in.

If It's Really the Last Minute

Let's say it's the morning of the exam and, for some lucky reason, you find yourself with this book. Look over Section II in the practice tests. Familiarizing yourself with the types of questions the essays ask will give you a head start on figuring out how to respond to them. Also skim the section on multiple-choice strategies, paying particular attention to the footnote questions.

Checklist for the Night Before

Put together a backpack or small bag with everything you'll need for the test. Have it ready the night before so that you can grab it and go, knowing you're properly equipped. Here is what you might put inside:

- Several pencils and a good eraser (test it first to make sure it erases without marking the paper).

- A small, easy-to-eat snack. Avoid chocolate, which could melt and get all over your hands and your desk. Avoid nuts, which could trigger allergies in other testers. An energy bar, an easy-to-eat piece of fruit, or some crackers would be good choices.

- A bottle of water. Avoid drinks with sugar or caffeine. You may think they'll give you energy, but they're more likely to make you jittery.

Don't stay up all night studying. Get a good night's sleep so you will be alert and ready for the test. Eat a light but satisfying meal before the test. Protein-rich foods like eggs, nuts, and yogurt are a good choice. Don't eat too heavily—you don't want to be sleepy or uncomfortably full. If you must have coffee, don't overdo it. Dress in layers. You want to be able to adjust if the testing room is too warm or too cool. Wear comfortable clothes.

Test Day
- Don't bring anything you don't need. Cell phones, pagers, and anything else that might let you communicate outside the test room will be prohibited.

- Do bring a photo ID and your school code.

- Wear or bring a watch. If your watch has any alarms, buzzers, or beepers, turn them off.

Once you get to the testing room, take a few deep breaths and relax. Remind yourself that you're well prepared. It's natural to be nervous. Channel your nervousness into alertness and energy for the long test ahead. When the test begins, set all worries aside. You've done all you can to prepare. Time to make that preparation pay off!

A Brief Guide to the Multiple-Choice Section

You'll find a more detailed section on multiple-choice strategies on page 27. If you're short on time, here's a brief review of how to approach this section. You have 60 minutes to read all the essays and answer every question—not a lot of time. These tips should help you make the most of your precious time to get as many answers correct as you can.

Approaching the Section

Spend about two minutes looking over the entire section to identify the passages that look easiest. Start with those, and then move on to the more difficult ones. That doesn't mean you should read the shortest passages first. A longer passage might have more questions that you can get out of the way, and it may well be easier to read than a short passage.

Reading the Passages

- Read the passage before you read the questions—if you don't, you risk misconstruing the passage or missing important information.

- As you read, let the author engage your mind, and follow his argument carefully. Don't skim. If you're familiar with the topic, keep your own point of view out of it and focus on the author's arguments. Watch out for any rhetorical strategies the author uses.

- Take note of anything interesting by underlining, circling, or jotting words in the margins.

- Keep forging ahead. Don't linger long if you don't understand something, but mark the unfamiliar text with a question mark. The questions themselves might help you understand what the author is saying, or there might not be a question on that text at all.

Answering the Questions

- Some questions will ask about the passage in general. Start with those. When you get to questions that deal with specific parts, reread those sections and the sentence or two before and after.

- Answer the questions you know the answer to first. If a question stumps you, come back to it.

- If you're not sure of the answer, start by eliminating answer choices you know are wrong. In some cases, you can eliminate the answer choice that seems most different from the others.

- Sometimes two similar answer choices remain as strong candidates. One is the right answer; the other is an "attractive distracter." Focus on the differences between the answer choices and review the part of the passage that helps you guess which is correct.

- If you're still unsure, take a guess. There is no penalty for guessing, and you may have your best shot at guessing correctly now, when the passage is fresh in your mind. If it's a wild guess, mark the question on your booklet to come back to if you have time.

- Make sure you've marked your answers next to the correct item on your answer sheet, particularly if you haven't gone through the test in order. Don't leave any stray marks on your answer sheet.

- If you have time at the end, go back to the questions you were uncertain of. Change your answer choice only if new information or insight leads you to a different response.

A Brief Guide to the Essays

You have 40 minutes to write each of the three essays. The examiners allot you 15 minutes to read the sources that accompany the Synthesis question. Here's a crash course on how to approach and write each type of essay.

Essay 1: The Synthesis Essay

Reading and Planning (15 minutes)

- Read the assignment, focusing specifically on the topic you are asked to write about and the minimum number of sources you must use.

- Read each source carefully, critically, and completely, being sure to read the information that introduces them.

- Underline ideas you think will be useful in writing your essay, and jot down any first impressions you have in the margin. Make note of which sources you think will be the most useful and which will probably not, such as by writing a check or a question mark beside them.

- After glancing back over the ideas you underlined and annotated, create a thesis—a specific, arguable point—that you can support using only information from the sources. Make sure it directly responds to the prompt and that it is specific and focused.

- Identify the sources that you will use. You must use at least three, but don't try to use all of them. You're better off providing a deeper analysis of those you do use. If possible, incorporate the visual source (for more on the visual, see "The Visual" in this section).

- If you have time, briefly outline your main ideas. Include any outside knowledge you have that can support your ideas.

Writing (35 to 40 minutes)

- Once you have a thesis, write a clear but brief introductory paragraph (three sentences is plenty) that includes your thesis statement. Feel free to use language from the assignment in your introduction, but try to make your introduction your own rather than merely parroting back the words on the exam.

- If you laid out a structure in your thesis, such as a list of arguments you will make or ideas you will present, be sure to follow that structure in your body paragraphs.

- Include a topic sentence in each paragraph that summarizes your main idea for that paragraph.

- Focus on the sources in your writing, not personal experiences. You may also include outside knowledge you have about the topic to supplement the sources.

- Choose the most relevant language to quote, generally using your own words to lead into the quotations. Avoid long quotations, opting instead to spend your time and space analyzing the text.

- Be sure to engage the quotation in some way after you have cited it. This engagement should develop or support your topic sentence and thesis in some way.

- The last sentences of each paragraph should include an argument in support of your thesis. The end of the paragraph should make clear why the information and analysis you have included matters.

- If you can, include a counterpoint to your thesis from one of the sources, which you can then refute using other sources.

- Add a brief conclusion that extends your argument in some way rather than just restating or summarizing it.

The Visual

One of the sources provided for the synthesis essay will be a visual source. Examples of visuals that have appeared on the AP exam include photographs, graphs, political cartoons, and charts. Even though the visual is offered as one option among several sources, consider choosing it.

Why Choose the Visual?

We are surrounded by manufactured images, from billboards to television to the Internet. The AP examiners, and colleges, too, want to ensure that students know how to analyze images so that they are not merely manipulated by them. Knowing how to read an image critically has become as important as knowing how to read text critically, and the AP examiners want proof that you possess this skill.

How to Analyze the Visual

Visuals have their own rhetoric; thus, analyzing a visual is much like rhetorical analysis. In rhetorical analysis you read the passage and identify what seems important in terms of syntax and diction. You then analyze how what you have identified informs the author's meaning. In analyzing visuals, you proceed in much the same way. However, for the visual, reading text translates into looking at the visual and noting all that the image entails.

To interpret the visual, ask yourself these questions about the source as a whole:

- What exactly does the visual depict?

- What is the main image in the visual? Where is it placed and why?

- Other than the main image, what other details are included in the visual, and how do they add to the overall meaning?

- Does the visual make an appeal based on ethos (the authority of the artist or subject), pathos (emotional impact), logos (logic or reasoning) or a combination of the three?

- Who is the intended audience of the visual?

- What is the overall effect of the visual? Is it confusing? Clear? Sparse? Complicated? Sad? Inspiring?

If the visual has text, ask yourself these questions:

- What do the words mean?

- Where are they placed?

- Are some words written in different sizes or with different fonts?

- Does the text employ rhetorical strategies? If so, what are they and how do these strategies inform the meaning of the visual?

- What are the connotations of the text?

- What is the relationship between the words and the image?

If the visual is a chart or graph, ask yourself these questions:

- What is being charted or graphed?

- What does the chart or graph reveal/prove?

- What do the numbers or graph lines imply?

- What are we supposed to learn or realize after looking at the chart or graph?

Once you have annotated the visual in the ways described above, you must analyze what you see.

Essay 2: The Rhetorical Analysis Essay

Planning the Essay (5 to 7 minutes)

- Read all of the information that precedes the passage. This includes the prompt and any introductory information that is provided.

- Read the passage. Underline and annotate the passage, paying attention to rhetorical strategies, interesting diction choices, and syntactical structure.

- Identify the author's argument, if not stated in the prompt, and how he or she supports the argument.

- Formulate a thesis that makes an argument that responds directly to the prompt. It can be helpful to choose a two-pronged thesis, one that uses a conjunction to make two related arguments about the topic.

- Skim the passage again, underlining or circling any rhetorical devices and strategies that support your thesis.

- Brainstorm any relevant outside information you have about the topic, the author, or the context in which the author was writing.

- If you have time, create a brief outline that organizes your evidence from the passage and your own knowledge into main ideas.

Writing the Essay (33 to 38 minutes)

- Begin your essay with a clear but brief introductory paragraph that includes your thesis statement. Feel free to use pieces of the exam's prompt in your own introduction, but try to use your own words.

- Do not organize your essay by rhetorical strategies. Instead, begin each paragraph with a topic sentence that supports your thesis.

- Limit your quotations and keep them concise. Too many long quotations will leave the impression that you are padding your essay, and will limit the time you can spend on analysis.

- After each quotation or reference to the source, identify and describe the strategy the author has employed.

- End each paragraph by arguing how the strategy furthers the author's purpose. The end of the paragraph should make clear why the information and analysis are important.

- Try to include at least three supporting paragraphs.

- You can boost your score by including relevant outside information about the topic, the author, or the time period and other context of the piece.

- Add a brief conclusion that extends your argument in some way rather than just restating.

USING RHETORICAL TERMS

While the rhetoric terms listed in the chapter beginning on page 47 can be useful, they are not necessary to writing the Rhetorical Essay. What you will need to do is describe what you see as significant in the passage provided. You will then have to analyze the function of what you describe. Your analysis must relate to the thesis you have constructed.

For example, imagine that the following quotation is from a larger passage and that you have chosen the quotation because it can support the thesis you have developed.

"Being dead is one—the worst, the last—but only one in a series of calamities that afflicts our own and several other species. The list may include, but is not limited to, gingivitis, bowel obstruction, contested divorce, tax audit, spiritual vexation, cash flow problems, political upheaval, and on and on and on some more."[1]

You now must describe what is going on in the sentences you have chosen. Here is an example.

The author calls death "only one in a series of calamities." This phrase is humorous and unexpected because death is the last experience of our lives. By placing death alongside a list of other disastrous incidents that happen while we live, the author makes death seem less cataclysmic and only one of any number of unfortunate events that could occur in a lifetime.

In this analysis, no fancy rhetorical terms were used. The writer merely described and responded to what she saw occurring in the quotation. Using rhetorical terms might win you brownie points, but sound analysis and reasoning are what earn you real points.

---

1   Lynch, Thomas. *The Undertaking, Life Studies from the Dismal Trade.* New York: Penguin Books, 1997. Print

Essay 3: The Persuasive Essay

Planning the Essay (5 to 7 minutes)

- Read the prompt and the passage.

- Decide whether you agree or disagree with the author's assertion, or if you agree with his or her qualifications. Brainstorm examples and ideas that you could use to back up your viewpoint. If you are unsure which stance to take, choose the one for which you can make the clearest case with the most compelling examples.

- Review the passage, jotting down ideas in the margins and underlining arguments that you can refute, support, or qualify.

- Write a clear thesis that (A) states your point of view in response to the prompt and (B) is supported by examples you can provide to support your viewpoint.

- Create a brief outline of your ideas.

Writing the Essay (33 to 38 minutes)

- Begin each body paragraph with a topic sentence that summarizes a reason for your viewpoint. Test your ideas for their validity by mentally inserting the phrase "this is true because" before each topic sentence.

- Be sure to engage the reason in some way. This engagement should develop or support your topic sentence and thesis in some way.

- In the last sentences of each paragraph, include an argument in support of your thesis. The end of the paragraph should make clear why the information you have included matters.

- Add a brief conclusion that extends your argument in some way rather than just restating or summarizing it.

Practice Time

You've reviewed some easy steps to planning and writing each essay. Now let's try following the steps in practice, using a sample rhetorical essay. You will see how a sample student annotated the rhetorical passage, and then how the evidence in the passage was used to craft a quality rhetorical analysis essay.

Question 2

(Suggested time—40 minutes. This question counts for one-third of the total essay section score.)

The following is an excerpt from Mary Wollstonecraft's *A Vindication of the Rights of Woman*, written in 1792. Read the excerpt carefully. Then write an essay analyzing the rhetorical strategies that Wollstonecraft uses to convey her attitude.

AFTER considering the historic page, and viewing the living world with anxious solicitude, the most melancholy emotions of sorrow-ful indignation have depressed my spirits, and I have sighed when obliged to confess, that either nature has made a great difference *reluctance?*

5   between man and man, or that the civilization which has hitherto taken place in the world has been very partial. I have turned over various books written on the subject of education, and patiently observed the conduct of parents and the management of schools; but what has been the result?—a profound conviction that the

10   neglected education of my fellow-creatures is the grand source of the misery I deplore; and that women, in particular, are rendered weak and wretched by a variety of concurring causes, originating from one hasty conclusion. The conduct and manners of women, in fact, evidently prove that their minds are not in a healthy state;

15   for, like the flowers which are planted in too rich a soil, strength   *Simile* and usefulness are sacrificed to beauty; and the flaunting leaves,

after having pleased a fastidious eye, fade, disregarded on the stalk, long before the season when they ought to have arrived at maturity.—One cause of this <u>barren blooming I attribute to a false sys-</u>

20 <u>tem of education, gathered from the books written on this subject</u> <u>by men who, considering females rather as women than human</u> <u>creatures, have been more anxious to make them alluring mis-</u> <u>tresses than wives; and the understanding of the sex has been so</u> <u>bubbled by this specious homage, that the civilized women of the</u>

25 <u>present century, with a few exceptions, are only anxious to inspire</u> <u>love, when they ought to cherish a nobler ambition, and by their</u> <u>abilities and virtues exact respect.</u>

In a treatise, therefore, on female rights and manners, the works which have been particularly written for their improvement must

30 not be overlooked; especially when it is asserted, in direct terms, that the minds of women are enfeebled by false refinement; that the books of instruction, written by men of genius, have had the same tendency as more frivolous productions; and that, in the true style of Mahometanism, they are only considered as females,

35 and not as a part of the human species, when improvable reason is allowed to be the dignified distinction which raises men above the brute creation, and puts a natural sceptre in a feeble hand.

Self-
deprecation Yet, <u>because I am a woman</u>, I would not lead my readers to suppose that <u>I mean violently to agitate the contested question</u>

40 respecting the equality or inferiority of the sex; <u>but as the sub-</u> <u>ject lies in my way, and I cannot pass it over without subjecting</u> <u>the main tendency of my reasoning to misconstruction</u>, I shall stop a moment to deliver, in a few words, my opinion.—In the government of the physical world it is observable that the fe-

45 male, in general, is inferior to the male. The male pursues, the female yields—this is the law of nature; and it does not appear to be suspended or abrogated in favour of woman. This <u>physi-</u> <u>cal superiority cannot be denied</u>—and it is a noble prerogative! <u>But not content with this natural pre-eminence, men endeavour</u>

50   <u>to sink us still lower</u>, merely to render us alluring objects for a
moment; and women, intoxicated by the adoration which men,
under the influence of their senses, pay them, do not seek to obtain a durable interest in their hearts, or to become the friends
of the fellow creatures who find amusement in their society.   **Concession/**

55   I am aware of an obvious inference:—from every quarter have **refutation**
I heard exclamations against masculine women; but where are
they to be found? <u>If by this appellation men mean to inveigh
against their ardour in hunting, shooting, and gaming, I shall most
cordially join in the cry</u>; but if it be against the imitation of manly

60   virtues, or, more properly speaking, the attainment of those talents and virtues, the exercise of which ennobles the human character, and which raises females in the scale of animal being, when
they are comprehensively termed mankind;—all those who view
them with a philosophical eye must, I should think, wish with

65   me, that they may every day grow more and more masculine.

As a practiced test-taker, you can begin by reading the prompt and
seeing that the reader is asked to both (A) identify Wollstonecraft's
attitude and (B) analyze the rhetorical strategies she uses to convey it.
Next, you read the passage and annotate it. Notice that the notes tak-
en include both rhetorical devices and strategies (simile, concession/
refutation) and words that suggests Wollstonecraft's attitude (self-
deprecation, reluctance). The reader also underlines the language that
most clearly conveys the author's attitude, as well as some examples
of her rhetoric.

Next, formulate a thesis that you can support with the ideas you have
identified in your annotation. For the rhetorical essay, a two-pronged
thesis (a thesis that includes a conjunction of some type) is always good.
Wollstonecraft seems calm and reasoned as well as deferential to the
male audience that might be reading the essay.

Thesis: Wollstonecraft's attitude is reasoned yet deferential.

However, the thesis is incomplete—her attitude toward what? Clearly, she is writing about women's lack of rights and their treatment by men, so this should be included in the thesis. A complete thesis might be:

Wollstonecraft's attitude toward the education and rights of women is deferential toward men, yet also reasoned.

Now that you have a thesis, you must support it with main ideas. In order to do that, look for evidence to support it. This should include both ideas that support the author's attitude and examples of rhetorical strategies she uses. Here is an example of the notes you might take:

Key ideas—
* Society treats men and women differently.

* Women's education is neglected.

* Women are encouraged to pay attention only to their appearance.

* Women are not viewed as fully functioning human beings as men are. Instead, they are only given specific roles in society.

* The natural difference between men and women is made worse by society.

Rhetorical strategies—
* Simile: comparing women to flowers

* Juxtaposing "women" and "human beings"

* Polite and reasoned tone

* Conceding differences with men, refuting others

With 40 minutes or less to write this essay, you cannot address all the ideas listed. So, you need to choose the ideas that are tied to your thesis *and* tied to a rhetorical strategy. Here's how to do it. First, in the introduction, avoid meaningless generalizations.

In this excerpt, Mary Wollstonecraft discusses the lack of rights women experience in her society. This lack of rights is manifest in women's poor education and in their treatment by men. She approaches her argument by appealing to logic and presenting herself as a rational observer. Wollstonecraft's attitude toward the education and rights of women is deferential toward men, yet also reasoned.

Note that the introduction is brief. It is grounded in the excerpt itself, not in some generality about women, oppression, and sexism. The writer has made reference to rhetorical strategies, but avoided focusing on a single one in the thesis because there is not one dominant strategy.

Now let's read the rest of the essay.

Wollstonecraft believes that society has created an unnatural divide between men and women, with men assuming the favored position. The result of male dominance is that women's intellectual education is neglected. She states that "their minds are not in a healthy state; for, like the flowers which are planted in too rich a soil, strength and usefulness are sacrificed to beauty" (ll. 13–16). Wollstonecraft uses a simile to compare women to flowers. Flowers that are given overly rich soil in which to grow bloom too quickly, and therefore never develop sturdiness and longevity. Similarly, women are raised to attract men, but once their beauty fades, they are ignored or discarded, leaving them with little intellectual substance to fall back on. Later, Wollstonecraft states that women "are only considered as females, and not as a part of the human species" (ll. 34–35). Wollstonecraft juxtaposes "females" to "human species" to make the point that women are considered separate from human beings because they lack the ability to "reason." However, Wollstonecraft has pointed out that this is a false distinction. Women are not educated to reason like men. If they were, men would not be viewed as naturally superior.

Wollstonecraft attempts to strengthen her argument by acknowledging some differences between men and women. She defers to males' physical superiority and concedes that there are certain activities like "hunting, shooting, and gaming" (l. 58) in which women should not participate. However, she limits this concession by claiming that this "natural" superiority is exacerbated by men. "But not content with this natural pre-eminence, men endeavour to sink us still lower, merely to render us alluring objects for a moment"(ll. 49-51). The effect of this "concession" is to discredit the argument that women's lower place in society is the result of natural physical differences between men and women.

Wollstonecraft conveys herself as a rational observer who comes to her conclusions reluctantly. Throughout, she attempts to dispel the assumption that she is biased because she is a woman. She states that she has "sighed when obliged to confess" that society has likely made men and women more unequal (l. 3-4). This implies that she has not set out to make this argument, but was "obliged" to by the clear facts she has observed. The word "confess" (an admission made out of legal or religious obligation) connotes that she wishes she could say otherwise, but cannot. Later, she adds that she does not wish "violently to agitate" for women's equality, but cannot help but address it "as the subject lies clearly in my way, and I cannot pass over it without subjecting the main tendency of my reasoning to misconstruction" (ll. 40-42). Here, she indicates that she has not sought out this argument, but it has been thrust in front of her by the demands of reasoning. In presenting herself in this understated way, Wollstonecraft is acknowledging the reader's expectation of her as a passive, "ladylike" figure while at the same time arguing against it.

Wollstonecraft's arguments are based on her objective observations and her subjective experiences. However, as a woman of the 18th century, even her arguments are limited by the historical time period in which she lived. Thus, she believes that there are certain realms that belong to men only. As 21st century people, we now know that there is no realm from which women can or should be excluded.

Commentary

In writing the essay, the student has taken the key ideas and the main rhetorical strategies and woven them together into a coherent analysis. The essay is organized by main ideas, not by rhetorical strategy or the chronology of Wollstonecraft's essay.

Notice also the quotations that the student used. She chose a number of quotations, but selected only the text that was most relevant to her points. It's important to quote or paraphrase the essay as evidence to support your points, but you should also be economical with quotes to give yourself enough time for your own analysis. Be sure to follow the quotation with the name of the rhetorical strategy used, if possible. If it is just a particular word that seems significant, repeat the word you want to analyze.

Finally, look at the rhetorical analysis. The student not only described the rhetorical strategies used, but also explained how the author used them to advance her argument. When possible, the student gave names for strategies used (simile, juxtaposition, connotation), but at other times simply described the strategies.

THE MAIN COURSE: COMPREHENSIVE STRATEGIES AND REVIEW

If you have a few weeks to go before the exam, there's plenty of time to brush up on your skills. Here's a plan of what you can do to prepare in the weeks ahead.

- Start by taking a practice test to get used to the exam and the questions asked. As you go through the answers, note any areas of weakness. Read the answers and their explanations. The explanations to the answers are helpful in a variety of ways. Even if you have answered a question correctly, you might not know why it is correct. If you missed a question, you will want to know why so you can avoid doing so in the future.

- Carefully read "The Multiple-Choice Section" (page 27) to learn how to approach this section and know what to expect.

- Read the "Understanding Rhetoric" section (page 47) to brush up on your rhetorical skills. Memorize the rhetorical terms and learn the strategies.

- Review the chapters on essays (starting on page 73). Pay special attention to any areas of weakness you identified as a result of taking the practice tests.

- Take at least one more practice test before test day. You can download another free practice test online by visiting www.mymaxscore.com/aptests.

- A night or two before the test, go back over "The Essentials" for a refresher on test-taking tips. Do everything on the checklist on page 2.

- Pack you materials for the next day, get a good night's sleep, and you'll be ready to maximize your score.

The Multiple-Choice Section

The multiple-choice section of the AP Language and Composition Exam consists of 50 to 55 questions. You will have 60 minutes to read the passage and answer the questions. This section is worth 45 percent of your total score. It tests your ability to read carefully, closely, and critically. If you keep these three Cs in mind, you should be able to do well.

Scoring

In the multiple-choice section, you receive one point for each correctly answered question. Until 2011, you were penalized a quarter of a point for each incorrectly answered question. This is no longer the case. Therefore, you should strive to answer all of the questions, even the ones you really don't know. However, it's always worthwhile to improve your odds by eliminating answer choices you know are wrong.

Vocabulary

While vocabulary knowledge is important to scoring well on the test, it would not be worthwhile to provide you with a vocabulary list, as the vocabulary employed by the AP examiners ranges from the mundane to the esoteric. (If you don't know what *esoteric* means, look it up!) If you have time on your hands, review the list of vocabulary words for the SAT. You can find these online or in an SAT review book. Pay attention to adjectives that could describe an author's tone or attitude. Some common tone/attitude words are *bitter, condescending, contemplative, contemptuous, choleric, caustic, disdainful, derisive, erudite, patronizing, reverent, ridiculing,* and *sardonic.*

Focusing on the Text

You **must** read the passage before you begin to answer the multiple-choice questions. The passage must inform your responses to the multiple-choice questions; the questions should not inform your reading of the text. If you read the questions first, you might find yourself skimming the text for the answer. You then run the risk of overlooking key information.

Keep in mind that the multiple-choice questions are based solely on the text as it exists on the page in front of you. Do not impose your own views or external knowledge onto the text. If you impose your own views, ideas, or knowledge onto the text, you risk ignoring what the author is saying. What the text says is important; what you want it to say is irrelevant. You must read the text with an open mind, allowing what it says to inform your answers.

Clues from the Prompt

Typically, the passages will be from a different century, and we don't mean the twentieth. Some of the language may be archaic and/or include unfamiliar vocabulary. The passages are presented with little to no context. Thus, you won't necessarily know when the passage was written, why it was written, or who wrote it. If this information is given, pay attention to it. It will probably read something like this:

Example 1: This passage is taken from an eighteenth-century essay about the environment.

Example 2: This passage is taken from an autobiographical work written in the nineteenth century.

In the first example, the subject of the essay and the century in which it was written are given: eighteenth century, the environment. When you read the passage and answer the questions, keep the subject in mind. If you find yourself choosing an answer that has little to do with the subject, you might want to rethink your choice. If your answer still strikes you as correct, then go for it. In addition, the fact that the passage is from the eighteenth century should alert you to the possibility that familiar words might have unfamiliar connotations and denotations.

In the second example, you are told the type of work from which the passage is taken—an autobiography. Autobiographies are written in the first person and typically contain subjective observations and anecdotal accounts. The passage will probably be about a particular event that the author found significant or important in some way. Your job is to figure out what that event was and why it had significance or importance for the author.

The Three Cs

Reading critically, carefully, and closely requires that you read with a pen in your hand. For many students, underlining and making marginal notes while reading is a foreign and uncomfortable prospect. Get over it! You have a limited amount of time in which to read and answer the questions. Each minute counts. If you do not have to search the text for an answer because you have already marked it, you will save time. Underline what you think is important. Circle words that you think are significant. In the margins, include your responses as you read.

Reading critically means that letting the text engage your mind as you read. This engagement should take the form of writing notes in the margins. If something seems odd or unclear, you might write a question mark, whereas an exclamation point might signal that the author wrote something funny or unexpected. Use the form of annotation that comes most naturally to you.

Reading carefully means paying close attention to the author's word choice to ensure that you do not misconstrue meaning. Don't skim the text. The passage on the exam is chosen not only for its length but also because it contains enough information with which to generate questions. Reading carefully allows you to unpack the information it provides. Again, marginal notes and annotations are important here as well.

Reading closely does not mean holding the passage up to your nose! Reading closely is much like reading carefully. There is no real separation between the two. However, for our purposes, reading closely entails annotating the rhetorical strategies the author may be using. This may include, but is not limited to, devices such as asyndeton, polysyndeton, loose sentences, and others. Look for patterns, motifs and repetitions that might indicate the author's attitude or the tone of the passage as a whole.

To sum up: **Think. Use your pencil to underline and annotate. Leave yourself out.**

The Attractive Distracter

As you well know by now, the multiple-choice section of the exam tests your ability to read critically, carefully, and closely. In order to test how good you are at this skill, the examiners often include answer choices that vary only slightly. The answer that reads as though it might be correct is an attractive distracter. It distracts you from the correct answer. Thus, the difference between an attractive distracter and the correct answer is subtle. The bad news is that sometimes none of the answers seem quite accurate. In this case, your job is to choose the answer that **best** answers the question.

The attractive distracter functions a lot like the boy or girl whom you date even though you know he or she is bad for you. The attractive distracter shakes, shimmies, and flexes its muscles. Its appeal is so powerful, it is difficult to resist its charm. Be strong. Do not choose it. It is wrong.

You will know when you have encountered one of these attractive distracters if you have eliminated all but two choices, and these choices look almost the same. It is your job to figure out where the difference lies. It could be in connotation—the hidden meaning implied by the word. It could be denotation—what the word actually means. It could be a matter of implication. Consider context. Regardless of where the difference lies, these are frustrating answer choices because they are so similar. If all else fails, just dive in and make a choice. However, think about the choices in as many different ways as you can so that your choice is as informed as it can be.

Types of Questions

Overview Questions

Before taking the exam, it is useful to have a working knowledge of the types of questions you will encounter and what these questions are asking. Typically, the questions refer to the passage in chronological order. Thus, the first question will never ask you about a detail that appears in the last paragraph of the passage. Typically, it asks an overview question—a question that asks about the passage as a whole. (At times, the last question may also be an overview question.) Here are a few examples.

- The speaker in the passage is best be described as...

- The author's attitude is best be described as...

- The passage as a whole is best described as...

- The author's tone in the passage is best described as...

The first thing to note is the phrase "best described as." This phrase implies that the correct answer will not be an exact fit. The correct answer will be the closest or most likely answer to the question. In these types of questions, you will not find a choice that corresponds exactly to with what the question asks. In addition, all of the above questions are asking you to consider the entire passage before you choose an answer.

Attitude and Tone

Overview questions frequently focus on attitude and tone. The words "attitude" and "tone" have come to mean nearly the same thing. "Attitude" is the author's position on the subject. The author's "attitude" is revealed through "tone." For example, if the passage is a satire, the tone could be ironic or mocking. You can identify the tone and, by extension, the author's attitude by focusing on word choice (diction) and how the author seems to approach the subject. Frequently, the answer choices will include a pair of descriptive words: sympathetic yet critical, reverent and respectful, sanctimonious and condescending, feigned indignation, cruel indifference, mock serious.

Two other types of overview questions are the "except" question and the question that provides three or four choices. In this type of question, you must figure out which combination of sources applies. These questions are difficult because, again, they often ask you to consider the passage or a particular paragraph as a whole. However, these questions can also deal with only a few lines of text.

In paragraph 2, the speaker employs all of the following EXCEPT

A. concrete diction
B. parallel structure
C. analogy
D. simile
E. understatement

> The author's style is characterized by
>
> I.   technical diction
> II. condescending tone
> III. parallel syntax
>
> A.   I only
> B.   II only
> C.   I and II
> D.   III only
> E.   I, II and III

Organization Questions

These questions can focus on the passage as a whole, or can be about a particular paragraph. Here are a few examples.

- The principal contrast employed by the author in the passage is between…

- Paragraph 2 moves from…

- The structure of lines 59–68 can best be described as…

- The development of the passage can best be described as…

- The style of the passage is best characterized as…

Like the questions on tone, these questions might provide you with answer choices made up of pairs. Some of these questions require you to consider how sentences flow one from the other. Do sentences contrast with each other? Do they move from the particular to the general, or from the general to the specific? Does the passage have a thesis followed by supporting evidence? Does it have chronological development?

Questions of Style

Style questions can include a wide variety of answers. Again, knowledge of vocabulary is essential. The author's style is the way in which the particular passage is written. The following is a sampling of what you might encounter in answers to these questions:

- **Satirical writing** uses wit to point out the flaws and foibles of society/humanity to effect change.

- **Informal writing** is casual and uses language more suitable to everyday speech than to the written word.

- **Symbolic writing** is meant to represent or point to something other than the literal meaning of the passage.

- **Pedantic writing** is overly formal and sometimes includes the ostentatious use of language.

- **Didactic writing** is meant to instruct or provide advice.

- **Descriptive writing** includes specific details that often appeal to the five senses.

- **Abstract writing** is based on general principals and theories rather than specific examples or instances.

- **Technical writing** relates to a particular science, field, or profession and may contain industry-specific jargon.

Purpose and Main-Idea Questions

These questions ask you to identify why the author is writing the passage or what the central idea is in the passage. Believe it or not, sometimes an author's purpose is difficult to discern. You will have to ask yourself why the author is addressing that particular subject, how the subject is developed, and what types of evidence the author employs. Purposes can vary widely: to inform, to justify, to rationalize. Main-idea questions are straightforward. The examiners want you to identify the most important idea or point of the passage as a whole. To figure this out, look for an idea the author keeps returning to, one that is relevant to each paragraph of the passage.

Vocabulary in Context Questions

When a question asks you to identify the meaning of a word in context, your understanding of the meaning of that word may be irrelevant. The implication of this question is that either the word's connotation or its denotation is not the one that is most commonly understood. Connotations are how the word has come to be understood; denotation is the dictionary definition of the word. Thus, in order to answer these questions correctly, you will have to consider the words, phrases, and sentences that precede and follow the word as well as the sentence in which the word appears.

Strategy Questions

Strategy questions ask why the author has made a particular choice in a passage or sentence. These questions can also ask you to identify the strategy that the author has employed. This can be a rhetorical strategy such as abstract diction, catalogue, metaphor, or parallel syntax. It can include questions about appeals—logos, ethos, pathos—as well as questions about rhetorical fallacies: bandwagon, *ad hominem*, or appeal to tradition. If you are unfamiliar with any of these, look at their definitions in the section on rhetoric on page 47.

Inference and Implication Questions

An inference is something that you, the reader, do. It is a conclusion you draw based on evidence in the text. An implication is what the text, itself, does. It is a conclusion that the author wants you to draw by providing clues. Questions about inference and implication are typically worded as follows:

- The implication of lines 4–8 is…

- From lines 12–16 you can infer that…

Meaning Questions

Meaning questions are often followed by that tricky and irritating phrase "best expressed." This means that the answer will not be an exact fit.

Typically these questions refer to a few lines from the passage. The question will ask you to choose what you think is the literal meaning of the passage. In this way, these questions differ from the inference or implication questions because the meaning should be overtly stated in the text itself; you should not necessarily have to infer what the text means.

Grammar Questions

Grammar questions ask about grammar—no surprise here. For example, these questions might ask you to identify the antecedent to which a pronoun refers. The questions would look something like: "In line 47, what does 'it' refer to?" You will need to trace the pronoun back until you hit upon the word that makes the most sense as an antecedent. You might also have a question about which word modifies another. For example: "Which of the following modifies the word 'statement' in line 2?" Again, it is not possible to cover all the forms this question might take, so just be aware that grammar questions are also fair game on the exam.

Footnote Questions

Footnote questions are fairly new to the AP Language and Composition Exam. Footnotes indicate scholarship, and the AP is a scholarly exam; therefore, the examiners feel students should recognize the importance of footnotes and understand what the footnotes state. You can expect multiple-choice questions that ask you to analyze the information provided in footnotes.

Footnotes provide information that the author feels is important and believes the reader may not know. Footnotes also provide a record of the author's research so that the reader can check the author's sources and know from where the author has derived his or her ideas. Thus, footnotes help distinguish between the author's ideas and the ideas that have influenced the author. Footnotes can also include a digression that the author feels is interesting but perhaps not sufficiently relevant to be included in the main text.

There are two odd terms used in footnotes that you might not know. One is *Ibid.*, which is short for the Latin word *ibidem*, which means "the same place." It is the term used to indicate that the citation in the footnote is from the same source as the one that has preceded it.

> 1: Michael Henderson, *The Forgiveness Factor: Stories of Hope in a World of Conflict* (London: Grosvenor Books, 1996), 28–54.
>
> 2: *Ibid.*, 17.

Footnote 1 tells you that the work referenced by the author of the main text is by Michael Henderson. The name of Henderson's book follows. The information in the parentheses indicates where the book was published, by whom and when. The numbers outside the parentheses indicate the pages in the source where the information is found. The "Ibid." that follows in footnote 2 indicates that all of the information provided in footnote 1 is the same for footnote 2, except this time the relevant page number is 17.

The second odd term you may encounter in footnotes is *op. cit.* This term is short for the Latin *opus citatum/opere citato*. It means the work referred to in the footnote has been previously cited. Thus, *op. cit.* is used for a second or later mention of a work when intervening entries have appeared. For example, there might be 15 more footnotes before Henderson appears again. If the reference is the same as the one indicated in footnote 1, then the entry might look like this:

> 18 Henderson, M. *op. cit.* 24–25

If the author finds it necessary, he or she might also include the title of the book in the *op.cit.* reference.

Other Question Types

The above is not an exhaustive list of all the types of questions you will encounter on the exam. The authors of the exam are intelligent and cunning people. They can devise countless questions with which to interest, irritate, or confuse you. However, the list covers most of the types of questions that typically appear on the exam. Other questions on the exam will be variations on these question types, so this general introduction will help you.

Multiple-Choice Practice

While it helps to know the question types and some strategies for answering them, perhaps the best way to incorporate this knowledge is to practice. Use the strategies described to read and annotate the passage and answer the questions. When you have finished, read the analysis of the question and the answers.

Directions: Read the following passage carefully before you choose your answers. This passage is taken from a speech Queen Elizabeth I gave to her troops.

My loving people, we have been persuaded by some, that are careful of our safety, to take heed how we commit ourselves to armed multitudes, for fear of treachery; but I assure you, I do not desire to live to distrust my faithful and loving people. Let tyrants fear; I have always so behaved
5   myself that, under God, I have placed my chiefest strength and safeguard in the loyal hearts and good will of my subjects. And therefore, I am come amongst you at this time, not as for my recreation or sport, but being resolved, in the midst and heat of the battle, to live or die amongst you all; to lay down, for my God, and for my kingdom, and for my people,
10 my honor and my blood, even the dust. I know I have but the body of a weak and feeble woman; but I have the heart of a king, and of a king of

England, too; and think foul scorn that Parma[1] or Spain, or any prince of Europe, should dare to invade the borders of my realms: to which, rather than any dishonor should grow by me, I myself will take up arms, I myself 15 will be your general, judge, and rewarder of every one of your virtues in the field. I know already, by your forwardness, that you have deserved rewards and crowns; and We do assure you, on the word of a prince, they shall be duly paid you. In the mean my lieutenant general[2] shall be in my stead, than whom never prince commanded a more noble and worthy 20 subject; not doubting by your obedience to my general, by your concord in the camp, and by your valor in the field, we shall shortly have a victory over the enemies of my God, of my kingdom, and of my people.

---

1   Parma is a reference to the duke of Parma, in Italy. At the time of this speech, he is preparing to invade England under the King of Spain's command.

2   Robert Dudley, the Earl of Leicester. He was a particular favorite and close friend of Elizabeth's until his death. For many years he was a suitor for the Queen's hand. It was thought that he and Elizabeth were lovers.

1. The speech is characterized by

    A. scolding and rebuke
    B. self-praise and egotism
    C. reassurance and encouragement
    D. pessimism and gloom
    E. condescension and sanctimoniousness

2. The sentence that begins with "Let tyrants fear" (l. 4) does all of the following EXCEPT

    A. deny any tyranny on the part of the queen

    B. imply that the queen's actions are informed by the character of her subjects

    C. hint that the queen may become a tyrant should her subjects fail her

    D. underline the queen's regard for her people

    E. reveal the queen's belief that there is a power higher than her own

3. The speaker refers to "recreation or sport" (l. 7) primarily to

    A. show that she would abandon her leisure activities to support her troops

    B. compare battle to a kind of dangerous game.

    C. imply that victory over Spain will be easily achieved

    D. demonstrate her seriousness of purpose

    E. reveal her priorities as a queen

4. The footnote in line 12 explains

    A. the metonymic reference to Parma

    B. the meaning of the Italian/Spanish alliance

    C. the history of the Spanish/English war

    D. the Italian influence in Spain

    E. the existing invasion of England by Spain

5. The rhetorical device in line 9 is

    A. paradox

    B. anaphora

    C. polysyndeton

    D. metaphor

    E. synecdoche

6. The sentence in ll. 16–18 ("I know...paid you") implies that

    A.   Elizabeth will not pay the troops unless they defeat Spain

    B.   there is not enough money to pay the troops

    C.   honor and victory will be the only payment the troops receive

    D.   the troops feel they have not been paid what they are owed

    E.   it is a prince to whom the troops must appeal for money

7. The word "concord" (l. 20) means

    A.   harmony

    B.   aggression

    C.   pleasure

    D.   pugilism

    E.   bellicosity

8. Footnote 2 provides information about

I.   the identity of the speaker's lieutenant general

II.   the birthplace of the lieutenant general

III. the relationship between the lieutenant general and Elizabeth

    A.   I only

    B.   II only

    C.   I and II

    D.   I and III

    E.   I, II, and III

9. The speaker is best characterized as

    A.   humble yet sanctimonious

    B.   self-deprecating but assertive

    C.   arrogant and aggressive

    D.   resolute yet apologetic

    E.   pious yet secular

10. The passage develops mainly through the use of

    A.   contrast and parallelism

    B.   analogy and metaphor

    C.   logical appeal and intellectualism

    D.   hearsay and rumor

    E.   symbolism and allusion

Answers and Explanations

Initial Observations

First of all, you should have noted that Elizabeth is speaking to her troops. It seems safe to assume that they may be about to engage in battle. Why would a monarch give a speech to her troops? Perhaps she is trying to inspire them, buoy up their spirits, and encourage them. You should have also noticed the date of the speech. The speech is from the 1500's. As a result, words might have definitions other than how we, the modern reader, might define them.

1. C. This is an example of an overview question. Your knowledge of vocabulary and your impression of the passage as a whole will come in handy here. You are probably familiar with the word *scolding*. A rebuke is a criticism or a reprimand similar to but harsher than a scolding. There is nothing in the speech to support answer A. The fact that the speaker would lay down her life for her people (ll. 8–9) indicates that she is not egotistical or sanctimonious. She places herself "amongst" her people (l. 8); she does not view herself as their superior, nor does she talk down, or condescend, to them. Therefore, answers B and E are incorrect. Answer D is incorrect because the speaker claims in lines 5–6 that she trusts her people and finds strength and safety in them. This is an optimistic outlook, not pessimistic.

2. C. *Except* questions are often difficult. It helps to engage the three Cs in order to figure out the various implications of the sentence given

in the stem of the question. The sentence is "Let tyrants fear; I have always so behaved myself that, under God, I have placed my chiefest strength and safeguard in the loyal hearts and good of my people." Unlike tyrants who rule through fear and intimidation, the speaker places her "chiefest strength and safeguard in the loyal hearts and good of [her] people." You can eliminate answers B and D based on the sentence above: she gains her strength from and feels safe due to "the loyal hearts and good of [her] people." You can eliminate answer E because the speaker claims that she has "always so behaved myself that, under God." This reference to God revels that she believes there is a superior being watching her actions. In stating, "Let tyrants fear," the speaker implies that tyrants should take heed because she herself will never be one, so you can eliminate answer A. But this should call your attention to answer C. The queen never hints that she may become a tyrant, so this is the correct answer.

3. D. This is a meaning or denotation question. The speaker's point is that she has not come to speak merely because she enjoys it or because it is a source of entertainment for her. She has come because, as she states, she is "resolved, in the midst and heat of battle, to live or die amongst you all" (ll. 8–9). Dying in the heat of battle is a grim but realistic possibility. Elizabeth wants to convince her troops that she both understands the seriousness of their situation and would willingly experience what they might have to experience in battle: death.

4. A. Footnote question! The speaker refers to the duke of Parma as merely "Parma." Obviously the duke is not Parma itself but a representative of Parma, the city in Italy. When one term is substituted for another term with which it is closely related, you have an example of metonymy. E is an example of an attractive distracter because the footnote refers to the preparation for an invasion. However, a preparation does not an invasion make. Therefore, answer E is incorrect. The other answer choices can be easily eliminated as inaccurate.

5. B. Know those rhetorical devices. *Anaphora* is the repetition of words at the beginning of sentences. The speaker repeats "for my" to emphasize the fact that she has come to speak not for her own reward, but for others. No other answer choice is a possibility.

6. D. This is a tricky question because it is an inference question; thus, the answer is not overtly stated in the text. Also, your ability to answer correctly rests on your knowledge of what the speaker means by the word *forwardness* (l. 16). She states, "I know already, by your *forwardness*, that you have deserved rewards and crowns..." The implication of the word *forwardness* in context is that the troops have been bold and maybe even aggressive in their demands for payment. One only becomes bold and aggressive about payment if payment has not been forthcoming. Answers A and C can be easily eliminated because there is no textual evidence to support them.

7. A. Elizabeth is praising her troops, so by the context of "your concord in the camp," you can see that *concord* must be a positive attribute found in a troop encampment. *Harmony* is the only word that fits this description. *Pugilism* is skill in fist fights, and *bellicosity* is a warlike nature, two skills more appropriate on the battlefield than in the camp. *Aggression* and *pleasure* are not virtues in a camp setting.

8. D. The footnote clearly indicates the identity of the speaker's lieutenant general. He is Robert Dudley. It also provides information about the relationship between Elizabeth and Dudley—they were close friends and alleged to be lovers. However, it does not provide information about Dudley's birthplace. Though Dudley is Earl of Leicester, Leicester is not necessarily where he was born. Titles of nobility do not necessarily reflect birthplaces.

9. B. The speaker states, "I know I have but the body of a weak and feeble woman" (ll. 10–11). In naming her body as "weak and feeble," the speaker is engaged in self-deprecation; she is belittling herself. However, the

speaker is also assertive. She claims that she has "the heart of a king" (l. 11) and, "think[s] with foul scorn that…any…dare to invade the borders of my realms" (ll. 12–13). She threatens, "I myself will take up arms" (ll. 14). The heart of a king, scorn, and the threat to use weapons herself are all attributes of an aggressive individual who will protect her realm at any cost. Her use of the words "scorn" and "dare" underscores this aggression. Her point is that she has contempt for any who believe they are courageous enough to invade "her realm." These invaders will not succeed. Answer A and E can easily be eliminated as a result of what I have just explained above. Answer C might be an attractive distracter; however, the fact that she belittles her body precludes arrogance. It is difficult to be arrogant and self-denigrating at the same time. Answer D might also be an attractive distracter. The speaker is quite definitely resolute. She is determined and purposeful. However, she is not apologetic. Even when she refers to the fact that the troops have not been paid, she does not apologize. She merely "assures" them that "they shall be duly paid" (l. 18).

10. A. The speaker employs the conjunction *but* four times from line 3 to line 11. "But," like "however," introduces a statement that disagrees with what has been previously stated. Disagreements are contrasts. Parallel structure, or parallelism, means using the same pattern of words to show that two or more ideas have the same level of importance. This can happen at the word, phrase, or clause level. The usual way to join parallel structures is with the use of coordinating conjunctions. The speaker's parallelism is developed through the use of the conjunction *but*. On either side of this conjunction, her phrasing is parallel. Answers B and D can be easily eliminated because neither metaphor nor analogy exists in the speech, nor do hearsay and rumor. The speaker's language is concrete and her examples specific. Answer C can be eliminated for the same reason. She does not speak symbolically. She motivates her troops with abstract language by calling them "worthy" and "noble" and by referring to their "valor" (ll. 19–21), but these words are not symbolic in meaning.

Understanding Rhetoric

Rhetoric was once understood to be the art of persuasive speech. Today it encompasses all the tools of language used in speaking and writing. The multiple-choice section and essay question 2 in Section II of the exam require that you know the definition and function of rhetorical devices (also known as rhetorical figures), rhetorical appeals, and logical fallacies (also known as rhetorical fallacies).

The multiple-choice section includes questions that ask you to identify these rhetorical strategies in the passages provided. Essay question 2 asks you to analyze how these strategies are used and to what effect. This section of the guidebook will provide you with key rhetorical terms, their definitions, and how and why they are used. These terms have been categorized to help you understand to what aspect of writing these terms typically refer.

Rhetorical Terms in the Essay

The ability merely to identify rhetorical terms, appeals, and logical fallacies will only be useful on the multiple-choice section. For the rhetoric essay, identifying the terms is useless if you cannot explain their purpose in the essay. Therefore, merely memorizing the terms that follow and their definitions will not be all that helpful.

What is important, however, is knowing how these terms are used by authors to create meaning. Even if you forget the terms, you will earn a high score if you recognize what is going on in the text, explain it in your own words, and then analyze how it functions. For example, if you forget the term "anaphora," the repetition of the first few words in successive sentences, in your essay you can merely state: "The first few words in the sentences in lines 2–4 are repeated." You would then have to go on and explain what this repetition does.

Diction Terms

Diction means "word choice." How authors employ words and which words they employ make a great deal of difference in terms of the meaning they are trying to impart. **Never** state, "The author uses diction to…" Obviously authors use words in their writing, or we wouldn't be reading their work! The following is a list of words that describe the type of diction an author can employ.

Abstract   A word that signifies a general concept, an idea, or a condition that is intangible

Example *Truth, beauty, freedom*

Function We all understand these words in different ways; they have particular meaning depending on who we are. When authors use these words, they want the meaning to be ambiguous so that listeners/readers can fill in the definition that best suits them. This helps the listener or reader to personalize the author's writing or speech. The overuse of abstract words is not effective. Writers must also employ concrete words.

Concrete   A word that specifies what is tangible, something we can know with one or more of our five senses

Example *Table, salty, frozen*

Function Clarity is the number-one rule of effective communication. Without the use of concrete references, what we read or hear would be so ambiguous as to be meaningless.

Connotation The implied or understood meaning of a word and its association

Denotation The literal or dictionary definition of a word (Think *d* for *dictionary*)

Example The words *walk*, *stroll*, and *stride* have basically the same denotation, but *stroll* has a connotation of walking slowly or lazily, while *stride* connotes a more purposeful walk.

Function Authors can manipulate meaning when they play with connotation and denotation. To this end, authors must be aware of their audience, as each audience brings with it its own associations with certain words. For example, those who advocate for the end of a war will hear certain words differently from those who advocate for the escalation of a war.

Colloquialism Words and phrases used in casual conversation and given new, informal meanings, often associated with particular regions in the country

Example *Not the sharpest knife in the drawer; it's a no-brainer; open a can of worms*

Function Colloquialisms suggest a casual and conversational tone. They are used when the author wants to affect an informal tone and when the author wants the audience to identify him or her as one of their own.

Jargon

The specialized language of a professional, occupational, or other group. Connotatively, jargon has come to mean pretentious, wordy, and almost meaningless language.

Example *The heterozygous condition bears a greater selective advantage than either homozygous condition.*

Function Authors employ jargon correctly when they are addressing an audience made up of their professional peers. If authors use jargon to be wordy and pretentious, it will be your job to figure out if they are being satirical or serious.

Neologism

A recently invented phrase or word

Example I didn't know the Web address of his *blog*, so I had to *Google* it.

Function Changes in technology or culture often result in neologisms. With the rise of the Internet, new words such as *blog* were created, and proper names and familiar words were given new meaning, such as *Google* (to search online), *text* (to send a text message), or *tweet* (to post a message on Twitter). Neologisms are sometimes used to make an author seem up-to-date or trendy.

Archaism

An old-fashioned word or expression that has passed out of usage

Example *Ye olde tavern* is next door.

Function Authors use archaisms to suggest an earlier time period or style. Warning: Authors who lived in time periods one or more centuries before our own do not employ archaisms. Their language is archaic to us; to them, it is their language!

Syntax Terms

Syntax is sentence structure. There are a variety of terms that relate to how authors structure their sentences in terms of phrases, clauses, and word arrangement. "Syntax" refers to this arrangement. As with the word *diction*, you should never state that the author uses syntax. Without syntax, there would be nothing but a meaningless jumble of words.

Anaphora	The exact repetition of the first few words or phrases at the beginning of successive sentences or clauses

Example "*Go back* to Mississippi, *go back* to Alabama. *Go back* to South Carolina, *go back* to Georgia, *go back* to the slums and ghettos of our northern cities, knowing that somehow this situation can and will be changed." —Martin Luther King

Function Typically, anaphora emphasizes through repetition, but it can do more than that. The above example is taken from Martin Luther King's "I Have a Dream" speech. Through the use of the anaphoric phrase "go back," King reveals his understanding that his listeners have experienced oppression throughout the country. His repetition emphasizes this knowledge and the fact that his listeners can return to their homes secure in the knowledge that racial oppression will be eradicated.

Epistrophe Repetition of the same words at the end of successive phrases, clauses or sentences (also known as epiphora or antistrophe)

Example As an obsessive compulsive, I have difficulty knowing *when to stop cleaning, when to stop tidying, when to stop washing my hands, and when to stop worrying.*

Function Epistrophe emphasizes the last word in a phrase, clue, or sentence. In some ways, this is a more powerful emphatic device than anaphora, as what occurs at the end of sentences is usually what is most remembered.

Antithesis

The contrast of ideas by means of the parallel arrangement of words, phrases or clauses

Example *"It was the best of times; it was the worst of times."*—Charles Dickens

Function Antithesis functions to make a point regarding the contrast created. In the above example from Charles Dickens's *A Tale of Two Cities*, Dickens uses antithesis to bring a focus to the contrast between best and worst. The implication of the contrast is that the time period in which the novel is set encompasses both the best and the worst. How one experiences the time period varies from person to person.

Asyndeton

The listing of words, phrases, or clauses without the use of a typically occurring conjunction. Be warned: If a conjunction appears, even if the list is 17 lines long, you no longer have asyndeton.

Example When I stepped outside, I was bowled over by the smell. The air was filled with the smells of *smog, pollution, car emissions, burnt leaves, septic-tank stench, festering garbage, dead cat, putrid vomit.*

Function Asyndeton provides the feeling of a spontaneous and unconsidered reaction. It can also create a climatic effect through the cumulative buildup of the words, phrases, or clauses in the list.

Polysyndeton   The use of a conjunction after each word, phrase, or clause in a list

Example   They hated her for *her attitude and her appearance and her values and her political views and her family background and her current job.*

Function   Like asyndeton, the use of polysyndeton can also create the feeling of a spontaneous and un-considered response. However, unlike asyndeton, it emphasizes each word, phrase, or clause in the list, making each stand out. The conjunction provides a pause between the phrases in the example above, thereby emphasizing each reason why the speaker hates the girl.

Ambiguity   The purposeful creation of a statement with more than one possible meaning

Example   *I sense him. He is near. I can almost hear him. He is angry.* If you did not know to whom "he" referred, the ambiguous pronoun might create a sense of suspense and foreboding.

Function   Authors employ ambiguity when they want to create room for a variety of interpretations. If used well, ambiguity can enrich writing, making it more complex.

Inversion   A reversal of the usual order of words

Example   "And so my fellow Americans, *ask not* what your country can do for you—ask what you can do for your country." —John F. Kennedy

Function   *Do not ask* has been inverted to "ask not." The function of inversion is to emphasize the inverted words. In the above example, "ask not" is emphasized to make the point that we should not look to America to do for us, but instead, we should think about how we can make America a better place.

Parallelism

Parallelism, or parallel structure, means using the same pattern of words, phrases, or clauses in a sentence.

Example "The industry has repeatedly *denied* that problems exist, *impugned* the motives of its critics, *fought* vehemently against federal oversight, *sought* to avoid any responsibility for outbreaks of food poisoning and *worked* hard to shift the costs of food safety efforts onto the general public." —Eric Schlosser

Function The use of parallelism indicates that each parallel element is of the same level of importance. It also emphasizes these ideas. In the example above, Schlosser, in his book *Fast Food Nation*, lists through parallel structure the meatpacking industry's response to health concerns about meat. The list is long, indicating how much the industry has done to avoid responsibility. Further, the structure reveals the importance of each idea in Schlosser's list. As an aside, parallel structure is an important aspect of good writing.

Cataloguing

A fancy word for "listing"

Example See the example for parallel structure above. Schlosser catalogues the problems with the meat industry. Another example: I was impressed by his *wit, charm, good looks, intelligence, and sense of humor.*

Function The function depends on what is listed. As indicated above, the structure reveals the importance of each idea in Schlosser's list. Further, his list overwhelms due to the length and the breadth of the meat packing industry's refusal to deal with health concerns regarding meat and its processing.

Repetition

The repeated use of a word, phrase, or clause

Example During the holidays, all I do is *give, give, give*.

Function To emphasize. "Give" is emphasized to reveal that for the speaker, the holidays can be reduced to the act of bestowing gifts on others. This is not necessarily a positive experience.

Juxtaposition

The placement of two items next to or near each other

Example "With this faith we will be able to transform the *jangling discords* of our nation into a *beautiful symphony* of brotherhood." —Martin Luther King

Function Authors juxtapose words, phrases, or clauses in order to imply a correlation, to emphasize, or to make a point through contrast. The above example from "I Have a Dream" could be analyzed in a variety of ways, including to explain imagery. However, for our purposes here, King juxtaposes the "jangling discords of our nation" to "a beautiful symphony of brotherhood" to emphasize that if his dream of brotherhood were to be achieved, the nation's racial division would be eradicated. The result: a country united as one. Note: This example could also be considered antithesis, since it contains two contrasting ideas.

Aphorism	A concisely phrased statement of a truth or opinion

Example   "Money often costs too much" or "A friend is one before whom I may think aloud." — Ralph Waldo Emerson

Function The function of an aphorism is indicated in the definition; aphorisms point to a larger truth.

Chiasmus   Two or more clauses related to each other through a reversal of structures in order to make a larger point; the clauses display inverted parallelism

Example One should *eat to live*, not *live to eat*.

Function   Like aphorisms, the use of chiasmus points to a larger truth. When employed, it is a nice rhetorical flourish.

Loose sentence   A sentence in which the main idea (which is also main clause of the sentence) comes first and is followed by subordinate clauses and phrases that provide support for the main idea

Example *I knew I was lost since I was not familiar with the street names, did not recognize any houses, saw children I had never seen before, and was barked at by dogs that did not know me.*

Periodic sentence   A long and frequently involved sentence in which the main idea appears at the end

Example Unable to defend myself against the cold, the snow, the sleet, and the hail, *I lay down and waited for death.*

Rhetorical question A question to which no answer is expected

Example   "I ask gentlemen, sir, *what means this martial array, if its purpose be not to force us to submission? Can gentlemen assign any other possible*

motive for it? Has Great Britain any enemy, in this quarter of the world, to call for all this accumulation of navies and armies? No, sir, she has none. They are meant for us: they can be meant for no other. They are sent over to bind and rivet upon us those chains which the British ministry have been so long forging." —Patrick Henry

Function Rhetorical questions help to engage the audience and emphasize the answers that follow them. In the above speech, Henry asks a series of rhetorical questions that lead to his argument: The British are not to be trusted and will force Americans to do what is not in America's best interest.

Literary Devices and Figurative Language

Literary devices and figurative language are techniques or strategies used to create a specific effect or convey a particular meaning. When these are employed, the author goes beyond literal meaning to create a certain effect that informs the meaning of the work, passage, or excerpt.

Imagery
Words and phrases that evoke sensory experiences for the reader. Imagery appeals to what can be seen, felt, tasted, heard, or smelled. If an author employs imagery, it is your job to identify the type of imagery the author is using. Merely stating the author uses imagery is insufficient.

Example I could hear it now—my spurned lover, cast out into the cold, was banging once again at the door to my heart.

Function Imagery is most often used in works of fiction and poetry; however, as the definition indicates, when used in nonfiction works, images evoke sensory experience. An author can employ a controlling image to convey thoughts or feelings. A controlling image, like an extended metaphor, shapes the meaning of the work.

Allusion

An indirect reference to a historical event, literary work, or religious book

Example   "Mr. President, it is natural to man to indulge in the illusions of hope. We are apt to shut our eyes against a painful truth, and *listen to the song of that siren till she transforms us into beasts.*" —Patrick Henry

Function   Allusions assume a common cultural heritage and are used to evoke particular images or experience depending on what the allusion is. They also save time because much meaning is conveyed if the audience understands the allusion. In the above, Henry alludes to *The Odyssey* and to mythology. The sirens were tricksters who brought ships to their destruction by singing a song that enticed sailors to crash into rocks. Odysseus stopped his ship from suffering this fate by having his men put wax in their ears so that they could not hear the sirens' call.

Archetype

A symbol that is reputed to be rooted in the human subconscious. Also, something that serves as a model or pattern for other things of the same type; the epitome of something.

Example 1   In "The Rime of the Ancient Mariner" by Samuel Taylor Coleridge, a mariner commits a crime against nature. Stuck on a boat in the middle of the ocean under a hot sun, he is dying of thirst.

When he sees the beauty in nature, it rains. In this case rain is an archetype for redemption, the cleansing of the mariner's sin.

Example 2 Jack the Ripper is an archetype of the serial killer.

Function Archetypes function as powerful symbols and examples.

Symbol

Something that represents or suggests something other than what it is literally

Example The wedding band on a man's or woman's ring finger typically symbolizes marriage. However, today, this ring can symbolize a commitment between two people, indicating that these individuals are off the market as far as shopping for mates goes.

Function Symbols are usually employed in works of fiction and poetry. In nonfiction works, symbols, like archetypes, can be used to communicate an idea or concept.

Caricature

An exaggeration that is often unrealistic and sometimes comical

Example Many political cartoons rely on caricature. They exaggerate the features of a political figure. For example, if a famous woman were to have her mouth emphasized, it might be because she has gossiped or been untactful.

Function Caricature draws attention to and can emphasize a certain aspect or quality of a person

Euphemism

Nonthreatening language that is substituted for more explicit and possibly offensive words.

Example The town suffered *collateral damage* when the American bomb went off by mistake in a parking lot.

Function *Collateral damage* is often a euphemism for the deaths of civilians. In the above example, the use of "collateral damage" is much less shocking and evokes no images of innocent men, women, and children dying due to a misaimed bomb.

Irony

A contrast between expectation and reality

Function Irony is employed to surprise the reader or viewer. There are a variety of tools that the author can employ to produce irony. These are discussed below. There are three main types of irony. Only two, however, are relevant to the AP Language Exam.

Examples *Verbal irony*, which can include sarcasm when spoken aloud, occurs when the author says one thing but means another. Jonathan Swift's social satire, "A Modest Proposal," is filled with verbal irony due to the nature of Swift's proposal: that starving and unemployed Irish mothers and fathers should sell their children for food so that these children are not a burden to their parents and so that the parents can have a stable form of income. "I have been assured by a very knowing American... that a young and healthy child well nursed is at a year old a most delicious, nourishing and wholesome food, whether stewed, roasted, baked or broiled..." (Note the parallel structure and cataloguing. Consider how they function to impart meaning.)

Situational irony occurs when the reader expects one thing to happen, but something else actually occurs. Surprise endings employ situational irony. For example, let's say you hate dogs. You have always hated dogs. You have repeatedly stated you would never want to own a dog. Dogs smell. They bark. Rain or shine, cold or hot, they need to be walked. One day, you are in the park. A stray dog comes over and you fall in love. You bring her home. You try for months to find her owner. None appears. You keep her. How ironic!

Alliteration

The repetition of a sound at the beginning of two or more words
Example *"The silken, sad, uncertain rustling* of each purple curtain thrilled me."—Edgar Allen Poe
Function Alliteration makes connection between and among words. This connection affects meaning depending upon how the alliteration is employed. In the above example, the repetition of "s" sounds underscores the sound made by the curtain.

Onomatopoeia

The use of words that sound like their meaning
Example The thief *crashed, bashed, smashed, and mashed* his way through the brush.
Function The words themselves sound like the sounds the thief is making. Their usage helps emphasize all the noise made.

Hyperbole

An exaggeration or overstatement
Example I was so thirsty; *I could have drunk the entire lake*.
Function The function will depend on the hyperbole. In the above example, the fact that the

speaker claims that she could "drink a lake" indicates the intensity of her thirst.

Understatement   An idea portrayed as less important than it actually is
Example I was *a bit put off* when, the day after our marriage, my spouse told me he had a virulently contagious case of leprosy.
Function Understatement may be employed for ironic or humorous effect. In the above example, it should be clear that understatement is used for ironic purposes. Leprosy is a contagious disease that can cause permanent damage to the skin, nerves, limbs, and eyes.

Analogy   An extended comparison between two **unlike** things. It is similar to an extended metaphor and simile, but the difference lies in the fact that the purpose of an analogy is to make an argument or explain something unfamiliar using something familiar.
Example "Life is like a box of chocolates—you never know what you're gonna get."—*Forrest Gump*
Function To explain or clarify some unfamiliar or difficult idea or experience by showing how the idea or object is similar to one that is familiar.

Simile   A comparison between two different things that share some similarities, in which the comparison is connected by *like* or *as*
Example "The *wrath of God is like great waters* that are dammed for the present." —Jonathan Edwards
Function Like metaphors and analogies, the function of a simile is contingent upon what is being

compared. In the above example from Edwards's sermon "Sinners in the Hands of an Angry God," the simile compares God's wrath to "dammed waters." Like waters that are dammed, God's anger at sinners is building in intensity. At some point, the dam may give in and the rushing onslaught of water, like God's unleashed anger, will wash the sinful away. Note: You must always name what is compared in the simile.

Metaphor

The comparison of two different things that share some similarities, in which the comparison is made without the use of "like" or "as." Extended metaphors, metaphors that continue throughout the passage, are easily confused with analogies. However, metaphors are generally used to provide vivid descriptions rather than to explain something unfamiliar.

Example In "Author to her Book," Anne Bradstreet employs an extended metaphor to compare her book to a child. "Thou ill-formed offspring of my feeble brain, / Who after birth didst by my side remain."

Function The function of a metaphor is contingent upon what is being compared. However, unlike analogies or similes, metaphors state that one thing *is* the other thing. In the above example, Bradstreet compares her book to a child. By describing her "child" as an "ill-formed offspring," Bradstreet's metaphor implies that her book is not well written, coming as it did from her "feeble" brain. It also implies that the book, like a child, required grueling labor in its birth.

Metonymy	A term that is substituted for another term with which it is closely related

Examples *The White House* refused to comment; we've earned this by the *sweat* of our brow; he smoked a *pack* a day.

Function Metonymy may substitute the whole for a part, or a part for the whole ("The White House" for the president); the effect for the cause ("sweat" for hard work); or a container for its contents ("a pack" for cigarettes).

Synecdoche	Synecdoche is a relative of metonymy. Here, however, an actual part of the whole is substituted for the whole.

Example I want the attention of *every ear*.

Function As the speaker wants the attention of her listeners, she uses the word "ear" to signify the whole person. Ears are used to listen; therefore, ear is emphasized.

Paradox	A statement that seems contradictory, but actually points to a truth

Example "The more things change, the more they remain the same." —Jean-Baptiste Alphonse Karr

Function The function is as the definition indicates: to point to a larger truth or irony in a concise and thought-provoking way.

Oxymoron	A two-word contradiction

Example *Jumbo shrimp, ugly beauty*

Function An oxymoron is a more concise statement of a paradox.

Personification Human qualities given to non-human subjects

Example The tree *beckoned* to us with *her limbs*.

Function Like many of these devices, the function depends on the context. The example above personifies the tree to indicate that the author feels that the tree is calling to him.

Apostrophe The addressing of an inanimate object or an idea as if it were human.

Example Oh bathtub, you help me when I am stressed, worried, or concerned.

Function Much like personification, an apostrophe emphasizes certain aspects of the inanimate object or concept.

Styles of Writing

On the multiple-choice section, you may be asked to identify the style that best characterizes the author's work. Below is a list of some of the styles you may encounter.

Parody A literary work that imitates either the style or the subject matter of an author for the purposes of ridicule, criticism, or tribute

Satire A literary work in which the ideas, customs, behaviors, or institutions of society are ridiculed to effect change. Satires range from mild to harsh. Irony and exaggeration are the main weapons of satire.

Allegory A literary work that occurs on two levels: the literal and the symbolic. Thus, actions, characters, settings, and objects have symbolic, abstract meaning. The purpose of an allegory is to convey truths about life, to criticize social customs, or to teach a moral lesson.

Sermon	A religious speech meant to be spoken out loud and containing a moral or didactic lesson. *Didactic* means "intended to instruct, often excessively so."
Elegy	A thoughtful poem lamenting someone's death
Narrative	Any type of writing that is concerned with relating an event or a series of events
Anecdote	A brief narrative or a retelling of a story or event often based on the speaker's own experience.
Panegyric	A statement of high praise
Polemic	A passionate or strongly worded controversial argument against something or someone.
Diatribe	A bitter attack on something or someone. A diatribe differs from a polemic because a diatribe is totally against the subject of the diatribe. A polemic is meant to create controversy.

Rhetorical Appeals and Rhetorical Fallacies

Convincing arguments incorporate a variety of strategies in order to strengthen the argument being made. You have just read a list of many of the strategies authors can use. Rhetorical appeals persuade by convincing the audience of something about the author or by evoking feelings in the audience itself. A rhetorical or logical fallacy is an error of reasoning. When someone adopts a position, or tries to persuade someone else to adopt a position, based on a bad piece of reasoning, they commit a fallacy. A fallacy is something that is believed to be true, but is in fact erroneous. Rhetorical fallacies mislead and often purposefully so. The list below will be helpful on the multiple-choice section and for essays 1 and 2 in Section 2.

Rhetorical Appeals

Ethos	An ethical appeal that establishes the speaker's or writer's credibility and trustworthiness. This appeal is about the speakers or authors themselves.

Example Politicians evoke or elicit ethos when they attempt to convince the audience that they are honest in their business dealings and have the welfare of their constituencies as their first priority.

Pathos

An emotional appeal that stirs the feelings of the audience.

Example Politicians evoke pathos when they provide stories from their own background explaining how their parents had little, but still worked hard to ensure that their children were educated; how their baby brother died because their parents could not afford health care; and how they had to work 40 hours a week during college and graduate school because of a lack of funds.

Logos

A logical appeal or an appeal to reason. Writers or speakers use or elicit logos when they use logical and reasonable evidence to support their argument. This can include the use of facts, statistics, and expert testimony.

Rhetorical Fallacies

Non sequitur

Non sequitur is Latin for "it does not follow." In this type of fallacy the first part of a statement may be true, but what follows it is not true or even related to the first part.

Example *Those who do not support the war are terrorists.*

Analysis

For a wide variety of reasons, many may not support a war. This fact does not make them terrorists or even unpatriotic.

Ad hominem   *Ad hominem* is Latin for "to the man." This type of fallacy attacks the opponent not the issue.

Example *We can't hire him to teach our children; he was unfaithful to his wife.*

Analysis   Though a man's fidelity is certainly an issue of character, it has little to do with someone's teaching abilities.

Appeal to tradition   An argument that claims something should be done a particular way because it has been done that way in the past

Example *Because the Catholic Church has never allowed women to become priests, they should not be allowed to become priests today.*

Analysis   Perhaps the time has come to change church policy. What was considered sound policy in the past may no longer be considered sound.

Bandwagon   An argument that claims that since everyone is doing, thinking, or saying something, you should too

Example *All teenagers engage in underage drinking, so let's lower the drinking age to 18.*

Analysis   Not all teenagers engage in underage drinking. Further, even if most do, this does not make underage drinking right.

Faulty causality   The assumption that because one event follows another, it caused the other. The cause-and-effect relationship that is established is not based on sound reasoning.

Example *(Effect)* The dropout rate for high school students has significantly increased as of late. *(Cause) This is due to* the poor parenting skills of those responsible for these students.

Analysis	Though it may be true that drop out rates have increased, there is no infallible evidence that the rise in rate is due to faulty parenting skills. There is a wide variety of reasons for the increased rate.
Either/or fallacy	A statement that only two alternatives can exist when in fact there are more than two **Example** *If illegal immigrants are not ousted from our country, there will be no jobs for American citizens.*
Analysis	Though you may consider illegal immigrants a problem, their presence does not affect the availability of every job in America.
Inductive error	A conclusion based on too little or selective evidence **Example** *Big dogs are dangerous. I was attacked by one last week and needed stitches and a rabies shot.*
Analysis	Though the evidence provided is credible because it is based on the experience of the speaker, her conclusion is drawn from one experience with one specific large dog. Not all big dogs are dangerous.
Oversimplification	A statement or argument that leaves out relevant considerations. Oversimplification occurs when it is assumed that there is a single, simple cause of an outcome, when in reality it may have a variety of causes. **Example** *Gun violence can be eliminated if we have stricter gun laws.*
Analysis	Though stricter gun laws may help *decrease* gun violence, their implementation would not *eradicate* gun violence.
Slippery slope	A statement that assumes because one thing is allowed, other, more grievous, events will occur.

Example *If we allow gay marriage, soon people will want to marry animals.*

Analysis There is no reason to believe that if gay marriage is legalized, the next step will be people marrying animals.

Begging the question and argument from false authority

Begging the question is a thought process that assumes a statement's conclusion is true without any sufficient evidence to support the claim. Arguments from false authority attempt to persuade by referring to a person who is not an expert at all or who is not an expert in the subject under discussion.

Examples *Aliens must exist because there can be no other explanation for the many UFO sightings. Aliens exist because I saw a television show about them and people talked about their abduction experiences.*

Analysis The first example begs the question because it assumes that aliens are the only explanation for UFOs. No true evidence for their existence is provided. The second example appeals to false authority, because it is dubious that people who claim they were abducted by aliens were really abducted at all.

More on Rhetorical Analysis

Different types of passages are likely to employ different rhetorical strategies. Below are a few types of passages you may encounter and the strategies the authors may use within them.

Satire

Hyperbole

Mocking or condescending tone

Connotation
Irony: verbal and situational
Fallacies
Allusions
Neologisms
Humor of some type

Speech
Call to action
Appeals: pathos, ethos, logos
Anecdotes
Imperatives
Imagery
Parallelism
Concession and refutation
Anaphora, rhetorical questions, asyndeton
Allusions

Two Articles Side by Side Dealing with the Same Topic but Offering Different Perspectives
Logos vs. pathos
Statistics vs. images
Straightforward and factual vs. sensory-evoking diction/imagery

Personal Essay: Letter, Autobiography
First person
Emotional involvement
Rhetorical questions
Use of "you"
Ethos
Connotation

Writing the Essays

Section II of the AP Language and Composition Exam requires that you compose three essays in three different stylistic modes: using synthesis, analysis, and persuasion. Thus, understanding how to write the type of essay required by the prompt will be the key to your success.

For this section you are given a 15-minute period to read all of the sources for the synthesis essay. You then have 120 minutes to write three essays that comprise this section. If you do the math, that's about 40 minutes per essay. That's not a long time! You will have to get into the essay, make your points quickly, concisely and clearly, and then conclude as best you can.

The first step in writing an essay is creating a thesis, the debatable point your paper will argue. While each of the essays requires something different, there is one cardinal rule for creating the thesis for all of the essays: You must address the prompt. Failure to do so will result in a low score. Your thesis should also be specific and focused. (See page 81 for more details on writing a thesis.)

Essays 1 and 2 require that you use textual evidence to support your thesis. Without textual evidence, you will earn a low score. Textual evidence means using quotations from the texts provided to support your point. *How to cite and use text will be discussed in the section on quotation usage and citation.* Though your thesis is your opinion, your opinion's credibility rests on how well you can use the text as evidence to support your opinion. Whether you use the sources verbatim, summarize them, or paraphrase them, it is essential that you include and cite them.

The easiest way to organize your essays will be by breaking your thesis down into topics that will then become topic sentences. *Topic sentences are addressed in the section on "Supporting the Thesis."* Some students get right into writing their essays after jotting down a few ideas, while others first create a simple outline. While outlines take time to create, the time lost may be gained back if the outline helps you write your essay more quickly.

The 40-minute time constraints of the AP essays can be daunting. Few of us can write really well under this pressure. However, by following a few basic steps, you can learn how to get down three cogent, complete, and well-reasoned essays in two short hours.

The Basics of Essay Writing

1. **Create a strong, clear thesis.** This is step one after reading the prompt and reading and annotating the passage. How to create thesis statements for each of the three essays will be discussed more specifically in a different section. However, it is useful to keep in mind that your thesis must appear in your first paragraph.

2. **Watch your sentence length.** In elementary school and middle school, students are taught to combine sentences. This is fine when the ideas you are writing about are uncomplicated and unsophisticated. Mature writers vary sentence length and structure and are careful not to employ over-long sentences in their writing. Each idea must have its own sentence. If you have sentences that string ideas together with conjunctions, the clarity of your writing will be impaired. Short, simple sentences are excellent ways to begin paragraphs and end paragraphs. Short sentences are useful when they follow long sentences; they allow the

reader to process the ideas in the longer sentences. Short sentences also emphasize. If you feel that you are not a sophisticated writer in terms of word choice or sentence structure, don't worry. Clarity is what matters. It is better to write a clear, choppy essay than an unclear, rambling essay.

3. **Words matter.** Use them wisely and well. Multisyllabic, impressive (read: pretentious) words will not earn you a high score. Clarity and accuracy will. Use the vocabulary with which you are familiar to write your essays. Do not stick in words that sound good but say little. You can earn a high score on an essay that uses words that any one can understand. The readers of the essays are impressed by content, not by how the language sounds. Clarity holds true for pronoun use as well. Demonstrative pronouns like "this" and "that" are the bane of writing. Make sure there is a clear referent for these pronouns.

4. **Don't repeat yourself.** The readers of the essays are smart. They have good memories. You are writing a short essay, so any point you make will be remembered. Make your point once clearly and fully, and do not repeat it. This rule holds true for the conclusion of your essays as well. Conclusions should conclude, not summarize points already made. See "Conclusions" below.

5. **Write in the present tense.** This is the rule when you are writing about fiction and can therefore seem awkward when writing about some event that occurred in the past. However, it is best to write your essays in what is called the literary present. (Example: *Elizabeth resists Darcy's advances at first, but gradually comes to respect and love him.*)

6. **Organize by main ideas.** The essay should be organized by the main ideas you wish to convey. This particularly bears remembering for the rhetorical essay. It is often tempting to organize by rhetorical strategy—for example, focusing on tone, then diction. Remember, however, that these rhetorical devices are merely tools the author uses to achieve his or her purpose, and that purpose is what should ultimately drive the essay. To help focus each paragraph of the essay, include a topic sentence that summarizes the main idea.

7. **Supporting paragraphs should end with a "so what."** The end of the paragraph should contain an argument that ties the paragraph's points together and makes an argument in support of your thesis. Without a "so what" at the paragraph's end, the reader is left to wonder why you have included the paragraph in your essay. The reader asks, "Why do I care about this information?" Your argument at the paragraph's end provides the reason why the reader cares.

8. **Introductions should be concise and clear.** You will not have time to write long and involved introductions. In fact, you might want to write the introduction last. Longer introductions will be needed for the synthesis essay and the persuasive essay. Avoid rhetorical questions and generalizations. Though these are often taught as "attention grabbers," they do little more than elicit irritation on the part of the reader because they say little and waste the reader's time. Make sure that your introduction relates specifically to the prompt and your thesis.

9. **Conclusions conclude.** For some reason, many students are taught that conclusions summarize points previously made in the essay. If this were really the case, the conclusion would be called a "summary." The conclusion should supplement your essay's point in some way. Your conclusion can be a call for action or a change in attitude. It might be a discussion of what might occur should your argument not be followed. These are just a few ideas. You may have others. Even if you are running out of time, try to write at least one sentence that concludes in some way.

10. **Write neatly.** Those hired to read AP essays spend eight hours doing only that. They may lose patience with essays whose writing is difficult to decipher. Do not be one of those unlucky few whose essay earns a low score because of indecipherability.

11. **Focus on the evidence.** For the rhetorical and synthesis essays, focus on evidence that supports your thesis, most of which should come directly from the passage or sources. However, you can increase your score by including some outside information about the topic or the context of the passage. Just be sure the outside information is correct and factual.

12. Don't focus on the reader. Avoid assumptions about the passage's effect on the reader, or what the reader might be thinking. Even if you analyze a rhetorical appeal, explain how the author creates the appeal, not how it makes the reader feel about the author.

Example *The author evokes ethos and the listener believes he is trustworthy vs. The author evokes ethos by referring to his credentials as a pediatrician and regular churchgoer.* The fact that the author is a children's doctor and goes to church regularly inspires trust.

13. Avoid the pronoun "you." "In your response to a text, "we" is acceptable, as is "one," though "one" should be avoided if possible. "You" assumes a common experience. Your readers may not have had the experience you assume is common.

14. Don't expect perfection. The AP readers are well aware of the time constraints under which you are writing. They expect your paper to read like a rough draft rather than a polished product. If you spell a few words incorrectly or forget to include a few punctuation marks (or even misuse a few), this will not affect your score. The AP readers are assessing how well you respond to the prompt and how well you support your response. Though the mechanics of writing matter, if your mechanics do not impede clarity, you should do just fine.

Scoring Guide

Each of the three essays are scored on a scale of 1–9.

Scores of 8–9

Essays earning a 9 are similar to essays that earn an 8. However, 9 essays are impressive in the thoroughness and accuracy of their analyses and their use and control of the mechanics of writing. These essays have well-developed arguments supported by convincing evidence. These essays are not necessarily without flaws; however, the flaws do not affect clarity of argument or meaning.

Scores of 6–7

Essays earning a score of 7 are similar to essays that earn a core of 6. They resemble the top-scoring essays in that they respond to the prompts adequately, but less effectively than an essay that earns a 9 or an 8. Essays that earn a score of 6 or 7 lack the clarity and precision of the top-scoring essays. Over all, however, the writing contains only a few mechanical errors that may or may not impede meaning. Essays that earn a 6 have more mechanical errors than do those that earn a 7.

Score of 5

Essays earning a score of 5 are barely adequate. They address the prompts, but lack the complexity, thoroughness, and nuance of higher-scoring essays. These essays lack specificity and accuracy in terms of argument, evidence provided, or rhetoric analyzed. The writing may contain mechanical errors in syntax and diction, but, over all, the ideas of the essays are understandable.

Scores of 3–4

Essays earning a score of 3 or 4 attempt to respond to the prompts, but do so inadequately. Any argument made is superficial and less than convincing. Though some identification of rhetorical strategies may occur, there is insufficient analysis of these strategies or the analysis is incorrect. Some attempt is made to provide evidence to support an argument, but the evidence may be irrelevant or superficial. These essays reflect a lack of control of basic writing mechanics.

Scores of 1–2

Essays earning a score of 1 or 2 are unsuccessful. The flaws in diction and syntax affect meaning, making these essays difficult to follow. These essays may be vague or simplistic, or may misunderstand the prompt or the passages provided, thereby providing a response that is inaccurate. These essays rely on summary rather than analysis and argument. They provide little to no textual evidence to support the argument or analysis that is attempted. These essays exhibit a lack of control over basic writing mechanics.

Score of 0 or —

These scores are given to blank responses or essays that are off topic.

Thesis Statements

The thesis statement is the debatable point your essay will argue. It brings together the ideas that you will discuss under one coherent statement. While the thesis statement may be different from one essay type to another, every thesis in the AP test must obey one important rule: It must address the prompt. Failure to do so will result in a low score.

Another key to a good thesis statement is specificity. The goal of a thesis statement is to provide a focus for the essay, so an unfocused thesis statement will not serve its purpose. It should also be brief. If your thesis is rambling and vague, so too will be your essay.

What follows are samples and suggestions for writing thesis statements for each of the three essay types.

The Synthesis Essay

The synthesis essay provides you with six or seven sources, one of which is a visual of some type. The prompt asks you to "synthesize," or combine ideas from at least three of the sources, each of which offers its own view of the topic given in the prompt. These ideas must be combined to form a coherent argument that supports your thesis. **Ideally, you should include the visual as one of the sources to support your argument.**

The synthesis essay is much like a research paper. In a research paper, you find sources to support an idea. You may begin with an idea. You then do research and out of that research your idea is developed into a debatable point: your thesis. For the synthesis essay, you read the prompt and then the sources. From the prompt, you get your idea about the focus of your essay. After reading the sources, you develop your idea into a thesis.

Your thesis must be based on the prompt given on the exam; it must be specific and focused. The prompt is always preceded by introductory information that provides background on the subject. Be sure to read the introduction and prompt carefully so that you understand the purpose of your essay. If you do not, you will not earn a high score.

The synthesis essay is likely to offer one of three types of prompts.

EXAMPLE 1

Carefully read the following six sources, including the introductory information for each source. Then synthesize information from at least three of the sources and incorporate it into a coherent, well-developed essay that **defends, challenges,** or **qualifies** the claim that technology has had a negative effect on brain development.

This essay type, which is similar to the persuasive essay, asks you to take a position on a debatable claim (in this case, the effect of technology on the brain). You must decide whether to defend, challenge, or qualify the prompt's claim.

Defends: Agrees with the claim

Challenges: Disagrees with the claim

Qualifies: Agrees with claim in part or in certain conditions.

EXAMPLE 2

Carefully read the following six sources, including the introductory information for each source. Then synthesize information from at least three of the sources and incorporate it into a coherent, well-developed essay **that develops a position on** the importance of acting now to stop global warming.

This essay type is similar to the "defend, challenge, and qualify" prompt, but it is more open-ended. It asks you to develop a position independently rather than responding to a given position.

EXAMPLE 3

Read the following six sources carefully, including the introductory information for each source. Then, in an essay that synthesizes at least three of the sources for support, **evaluate** the relative importance of the factors that a school district should consider when hiring teachers.

This prompt is asking you to analyze and evaluate the various sources and develop a coherent viewpoint about them. Although the prompt is relatively open-ended, it is asking you to focus on something specific— the **relative importance** of the factors for hiring a teacher. While there may be other essays you could write regarding teacher hiring with these sources, you won't be responding to the prompt if you don't argue which factors are the most important.

In order to create your thesis, you must read all of the sources carefully. As indicted above, you must then take a position on the topic given. Your thesis must be a clearly stated argument about the topic. It will be informed by the sources given and your own understanding, interpretation, and evaluation of the sources.

Let's pretend the prompt is the following:

> Carefully read the following six sources, including the introductory information for each source. Then, in an essay that synthesizes at least three of the sources for support, develop a position about whether or not the federal government should provide funding for the arts.

Let's assume the sources include arguments for and against arts funding, a review of a public arts project, and a reproduction of an artwork. Here is an example of what a thesis statement might look like for this passage.

> Funding of the arts is an unnecessary government expense.

The thesis does take a position about public finding of the arts. However, it is vague because the reader does not know why the funding is unnecessary. More helpful would be a detailed thesis that gives an indication of the type of argument that will be made, and one that indicates that the thesis was developed by synthesizing ideas from the sources. More specific theses that deal with the complexity of the topic and the sources given might be:

> Funding of the arts is an unnecessary government expense that hinders rather than advances artistic expression.
>
> Governments should publicly fund the arts because doing so enhances the happiness and well-being of the public.

Both of these theses provide enough specificity to give a clear idea of the direction the essay will take. Be sure, however, that your thesis is not too specific. If your thesis states one reason for your viewpoint, you will be limited to that reason in your essay. This is fine if your arguments are all subsets of the reason you provide. If they are not, however, consider writing a two-pronged thesis statement that encompasses all the arguments or ideas you will offer in your essay. Here is one way the second thesis could be revised to encompass more ideas.

> Governments should publicly fund the arts because doing so encourages free artistic expression and enhances the well-being of the public.

If you find that you cannot create a thesis that encompasses all of your ideas without being unnecessarily vague, it probably means that you need to focus and limit your ideas to those that are more closely related. If you can't write a focused thesis from your ideas, then you won't be able to write a focused essay.

The Rhetorical Analysis Essay

Essay 2 requires rhetorical analysis. In order to earn a high score on this essay, you must be able to identify rhetorical devices and, most importantly, how they function to further or reveal the author's purpose. Though the prompts for this essay vary, they will always ask you to analyze rhetorical strategies as they support the author's purposes. Here are a few examples:

- Write an essay that analyzes how Edward Coleman uses rhetorical strategies to satirize the media's influence on Americans.

- Write an essay that analyzes how the rhetorical strategies that Anthony Armstrong uses reveal his values.

- Write an essay that analyzes the rhetorical strategies Phyllis Silin uses to satirize the shallowness of American consumer culture.

As a side note, analyzing satire is a popular choice of the AP examiners, so it's important to understand what satire does—it mocks social institutions or aspects of society to effect change or to point out flaws. Among its main tools are verbal irony and exaggeration. If you are unfamiliar with rhetorical strategies, go to "Understanding Rhetoric" (page 47).

After you have read the prompt and the passage carefully, being sure to take note of any rhetorical devices, it is time to construct your thesis.

Before looking at a specific prompt, here are some basic rules to consider when creating your thesis.

1. Do not list several rhetorical devices in your thesis. A good rule of thumb is to avoid the "laundry list" of devices. Thus, if the author employs more than three strategies, do not include them in your thesis. If there are one or two dominant rhetorical strategies, you are in luck. Create a thesis around these. Remember, your essay can analyze only the strategies named in your thesis.

2. If possible, try to complicate your thesis by inserting a "both, " but," or "yet." Examples:

- Sisson's view toward Cinderella is both contemptuous and dismissive.

- Sisson uses exaggeration and irony to reveal that she is sympathetic to yet critical of Cinderella.

These types of theses reveal a nuanced understanding of the author's rhetorical strategies. They are also focused enough to provide a direction for your essay, but inclusive enough to give you plenty to write about in your essay.

Here is a sample prompt, followed by two possible theses written in response:

SAMPLE PROMPT

In the passage below, from her book, *Cinderella: the Lonely Life of an Orphan,* Jocelyn Sisson discusses the character of Cinderella. Read the passage carefully. Then, in a well-developed essay, analyze how Sisson uses rhetorical strategies to characterize Cinderella.

LAUNDRY-LIST THESIS	SOUND THESIS
Sisson uses anaphora, alliteration, juxtaposition, and parallel structure to argue that Cinderella's refusal to confront the mean treatment of her stepmother results in meaningless self-sacrifice.	Sisson uses hyperbole and verbal irony to argue that Cinderella's refusal to confront the mean treatment of her stepmother results in meaningless self-sacrifice.

If, for some reason, you cannot create a thesis around one or two dominant rhetorical strategies, create a thesis that addresses the second half of the prompt only. The second half is the part that deals with the subject of the passage—Sisson's view of Cinderella. For example:

> Sisson argues that Cinderella's refusal to confront the mean treatment of her stepmother results in meaningless self-sacrifice.

If your thesis statement looks like this, in the body of your essay, you can analyze the various strategies Sisson uses and to what effect. **Note:** Avoid organizing your essay by rhetorical device. This subject will be covered more fully in the section on organizing your essay on page 91.

Now it's your turn. Let's continue the thesis practice by assuming that the passage has used juxtaposition, parallel syntax, and anaphora. The author's diction also plays a role, though you must specifically identify the word choices that are particularly important to the author's argument. Look at these three options for the best thesis statement:

1. Sisson uses rhetorical strategies to reveal the character of Cinderella.

2. Sisson uses juxtaposition, parallel syntactical structure, anaphora, and the words "optimist" and "martyr" to reveal that Cinderella's refusal to confront the cruel treatment of her stepmother results in meaningless self-sacrifice.

3. Sisson argues that Cinderella's inability to challenge her stepmother results in Cinderella's sacrificing herself.

Thesis 1 merely parrots back the prompt. Remember, a good thesis is a specific and focused argument, and this thesis is neither. The reader is left asking **what** rhetorical strategies are used and **what** is revealed about Cinderella's character. Merely rephrasing the prompt will not help you develop an argument, because you have not identified an argument to develop. Sometimes the prompt will tell you what the author uses the rhetoric to argue for or against, or what the author is trying to reveal. For example, a prompt might ask: *Analyze the rhetorical strategies Sisson uses to argue for equal pay for women.* In other cases, the prompt does not state the author's purpose. Regardless of which way the prompt is written, try not to merely parrot it back. You must work to engage the prompt and make it your own.

The appeal of Thesis 2 is that it includes rhetorical devices and identifies something specific about Cinderella's character. However, this thesis has the "laundry list" problem. Further, it may encourage you to develop your essay by rhetorical device, rather than by main ideas. Organizing by rhetorical device is a sure way not to earn an 8 or a 9. What is salvageable in this thesis is the argument about Cinderella's character; it is a specific take on how Sisson characterizes Cinderella.

Thesis 3 is the best choice. It avoids the listing problem of number 2, but addresses the key issue in the prompt—Sisson's characterization of Cinderella. This thesis lets you focus on your argument. You can then break this argument down into main ideas, which you will support with analyses of the rhetorical strategies the author uses.

The Persuasive Essay

This essay question can require that you do any of the following:

- Defend, challenge, or qualify a quotation about, or particular take on, a specific topic

- Evaluate the pros and cons of an argument and then indicate why you find one position more persuasive than another

- Take a position on whatever debatable statement is provided in the essay prompt

Unlike the other two essays, this essay does not provide any text other than the prompt. Instead, your thesis is supported by your own reading, observations, and experiences. In other words, this essay's only support is you; what you know is the "textual" support. This essay is difficult, as the question, regardless of what it is, presupposes that you have knowledge about the topic under discussion. The more you've learned about the world around you, and the more opinions you have formulated about it, the better off you will be for this essay.

If you choose to *defend* what the text argues, you will give reasons that support the argument given. If you choose to *challenge* what the text argues, your reasoning will contradict the argument of the text. If you choose to *qualify* what the text argues, you will agree with parts of the statement and disagree with others. Or, you might agree with the statement, but only under certain circumstances.

The "pros and cons" essay is similar to the "qualify" essay. It requires that you give reasons both supporting and contradicting the statement. You must then evaluate why one side is more convincing. The position essay requires that you establish a specific position in response to the statement in your thesis and support it.

As always, the thesis for these essay prompts must be specific and focused. Avoid merely repeating what the prompt states. Instead, make the prompt your own by articulating a specific argument. Take the following prompt:

In her 1999 book, *The Story of our Lives: What Fairy Tales Tell Us About Ourselves*, Jocelyn Sisson claims that fairy tales provide useful lessons for how to behave in life.

Think about the fairy tales you have read or watched. Think about what qualifies as a fairy tale. Then write an essay that defends, challenges, or qualifies Sisson's claim about the role of fairy tales. Use specific and appropriate evidence from literary, historical, contemporary sources, and/or personal experience to develop your position.

In order to create a thesis, you have to figure out whether you agree with the prompt, disagree with it, or agree with it in part. One thesis might look like this:

While some fairy tales teach lessons that can be applied to life, the majority present an idealized and distorted view of reality that does not easily translate to the real world.

What is this thesis doing? Is it (A) defending the claim, (B) challenging the claim, or (C) qualifying the claim?

The answer, of course, is C. The thesis agrees with the claim in part (in saying that some fairy tales teach applicable life lessons), but it mostly disagrees (in saying that the distorted reality of fairy tales is generally not applicable to life). This thesis could also be used for a prompt that asked you to evaluate the pros and cons of Sisson's statement. Your essay would first examine the reasons for your pro and then your con position. (Remember, you should always structure your arguments in the order in which they appear in your thesis, if they are specifically laid out.) You would then evaluate why you found one side more convincing.

Supporting the Thesis

No matter which type of essay you are writing, the body of the essay should include evidence to support your thesis statement. This evidence should be organized into paragraphs, each of which focuses on one main idea. This main idea should be summed up in a topic sentence that clearly supports the thesis statement.

The Synthesis Essay

Returning to the topic of funding for the arts, let's consider the essay that is written with the thesis, "Governments should publicly fund the arts because such funding encourages free artistic expression and enhances the well-being of the public." In writing the body of this essay, the evidence must be organized into main ideas that support the thesis. Each main idea should have its own paragraph and be summarized by a topic sentence that relates to the thesis.

Organizing the Body

To begin with the body of the essay, consider the thesis statement. It is divided into two sections, so the body should deal with the two parts of the thesis in that order. The first part to cover is "such funding encourages free artistic expression." You may have one or more paragraphs that relate to this aspect of the thesis—it depends on the evidence you have gathered. In your review of the sources, you might find several pieces of evidence demonstrating that funding encourages free artistic expression, and several more explaining why this is the case. Each might be covered in its own paragraph.

Each paragraph should have its own topic sentence. This is a general statement of the main idea. It should not cite specific evidence or use quotations. For your first body paragraph, the topic sentence might be:

> Public arts funding has been shown to foster free artistic expression in places where it might otherwise be hindered.

Providing Support

To support your topic sentence, you must give evidence from the sources provided. This can come in the form of a summary or a quotation. When using a quotation, select only the relevant portion of text, surrounding it with your own words when necessary. Be sure to cite the source (see "Source Citation and Quotation Use" on page 97). Here is an example of a body paragraph that begins with the previous topic sentence:

> Public arts funding has been shown to foster free artistic expression in places where it might otherwise be hindered. The *New York Times* article in Source C provides the telling anecdote of an artist who was forced to work at a restaurant when funding of the National Endowment for the Arts was reduced. "I went from producing a dozen big pieces a year to four or five, tops," the artist estimates, a reduction directly attributable to a lack of funding for his artwork. While some argue that public arts funding in the United States is too restrictive, the Center for Free Expression concedes that if public funding dried up, "a difficult situation would turn into a disastrous situation" (Source F).

Note the pieces of this body paragraph: a topic sentence that summarizes the main idea and relates back to the thesis statement, and multiple sources that support the main idea, including relevant quotations.

The Rhetorical Analysis Essay

When organizing the rhetorical analysis essay, it's best to organize by main ideas, not rhetorical strategy. The rhetorical strategies are simply the tools that the writer uses to achieve the goals of the essay, but those goals are what should be used to organize the essay.

You know you have a unified paragraph if you can summarize the main idea in a topic sentence. Usually, the topic sentence is at the beginning of the paragraph, but not always. Let's take a look at a body paragraph that supports the assertion that, "Sisson argues that Cinderella's inability to challenge her stepmother results in Cinderella's sacrificing herself."

Note that the thesis statement doesn't refer to specific rhetorical strategies. That's fine, and it allows us the freedom to organize by idea. Perhaps our annotation of the passage has led us to several instances of the author's use of rhetoric to portray Cinderella as submissive. Our topic sentence would summarize this idea, which would be followed by examples of specific rhetorical devices and strategies used by the author. Here's a start:

> Throughout the passage, Sisson emphasizes Cinderella's submissive nature, even when that submission is not conscious **[topic sentence]**. She describes Cinderella as "a hamster spinning on an endless treadmill" (l. 32). Through this metaphor, she demonstrates that what Cinderella sees as action in her own self-interest is, in fact, a futile gesture that gets her nowhere **[identification and analysis of rhetorical strategy]**.

Note that the rhetorical strategy is named and its effect is described in a way that relates back to the thesis. While you may find many rhetorical devices and strategies, stick to describing only those that support your thesis. Of course, if your rhetorical strategies support your topic sentences, and your topic sentences support your thesis, you shouldn't have anything to worry about.

The Persuasive Essay

For this example, we turn back to the prompt and thesis statement previously discussed for the persuasive essay.

> **Prompt:** In her 1999 book, *The Story of our Lives: What Fairy Tales Tell Us about Ourselves*, Jocelyn Sisson claims that fairy tales provide useful lessons for how to behave in life.
>
> Think about the fairy tales you have read or seen. Think about what qualifies as a fairy tale. Then write an essay that defends, challenges, or qualifies Sisson's claim about the role of fairy tales. Use specific and appropriate evidence from literary, historical, contemporary sources, and/or personal experience to develop your position.

> **Thesis:** While some fairy tales teach lessons that can be applied to life, the majority present an idealized and distorted view of reality that does not easily translate to the real world.

Unlike the other essays, you cannot derive topic sentences from the quotations you choose because no text is provided. Your knowledge and experience are, in effect, the "text."

This essay might otherwise be known as the "reason essay," because you must provide **reasons** to support your thesis. You may find it helpful to use the phrase "my thesis is true because" as a way into your topic sentence. Of course, you would not include this phrase in your final essay! For example, using the thesis above, you might think of the following reason to support your thesis:

> (The thesis is true because) Many fairy tales contain moral tales that are more simplistic than what we encounter in daily life.

For the final essay, you can use this reason as a topic sentence for one of your paragraphs. You would first eliminate the phrase "The thesis is true because," leaving the sentence that begins, "Many fairy tales...." You would then spend the remainder of the paragraph identifying fairy tales with overly simplistic morals, and explaining why they cannot be applied to real life.

Another topic sentence could be: (My thesis is true because) these lessons cannot be applied in real life. Again, your real topic would be "These lessons cannot be applied in real life." The paragraph might go on to illustrate the futility of applying lessons from fairy tales to real life.

Final Advice: The Concession and Refutation

If possible and if time allows, the synthesis essay (Essay 1) and the free response essay (Essay 3) should include a concession and a refutation. Identifying a counterargument and then refuting it is a sophisticated move that impresses the AP readers.

To concede means that you acknowledge an argument that contradicts or is counter to the one you have just made. However, you must then go on to refute the concession with additional evidence. To refute is to prove that the concession you have just cited is not true, or is outweighed by other factors. Obviously, if you do not refute the concession, you may undermine your argument. You will need to decide where to place the concession/refutation paragraph for maximum effectiveness. The two most common places for this type of argument are either before your conclusion or in the conclusion.

Let's say you use this thesis for the synthesis essay.

> Funding of the arts is an unnecessary government expense that hinders rather than advances artistic expression.

A concession and refutation would bring in a source that disagrees with the position you have established. The synthesis essay will always provide you with at least two perspectives on the topic given.

Let's assume that one source (Source A) claims that the National Endowment for the Arts funds controversial artists.

Your concession might begin:

> Though Source A argues that funding for the National Endowment for the Arts funds many controversial artists, this funding comes at a price—the funding results in a public outcry when politicians deem the art as "obscene" or otherwise lacking in merit.

You may also develop a point to concede and then refute in Essay 3, the persuasive essay. Here, the concession would be to an argument you might expect to be raised in response to your argument. You must then find an effective counterargument to this argument.

Remember that the concession and refutation is not an essential element, so if you cannot find a good counterargument to refute, don't worry—the most important goal is to support your thesis. However, including an element such as this signals to the test reader that you understand the complexities and alternative views to the argument you are making.

Source Citation
and Quotation Use

The AP examiners want to be assured that you know how to employ and cite sources. Almost all academic writing requires these skills. Further, these skills are foundational to any scholarly work, and the AP Language and Composition Exam is a scholarly exam.

In Essays 1 and 2, you must use textual evidence to support your thesis. Without textual evidence, you will earn a low score. Though your argument is, in a sense, your opinion, your argument's credibility rests on how well you can use the evidence from the text to support your thesis. Whether you quote the sources directly, summarize, or paraphrase them, it is essential that you provide citations.

Source Citation

Source citation indicates that you are including the words of another in what you are writing to support (or refute) what you are arguing.

There are many schools that have that have their own requirements for citing sources. Some of these schools are MLA (Modern Language Association), Chicago Style, APA (American Psychological Association) For the purposes of the test, it really doesn't matter which form you use as long as you are consistent. If you were to use MLA guidelines, you might cite a source as follows for the synthesis essay:

> The author states, "even cats and dogs can suffer from depression" (Source A).

Note the period goes outside the parentheses. For the rhetorical analysis essay, cite the line number(s) following a lowercase *l*:

> The author claims, "I was unable to walk. I was unable to move. I was unable to breathe" (l. 2).

If the quotation contains more than one line from the source, the citation follows two lowercase *l*s. (ll. 2–5).

Again, for the AP exam, it does not matter which style you use—just be consistent.

How to Use Quotations

For the synthesis essay it is important to remember that you are not a compiler of information. You are a writer. Therefore, it is essential that you **engage** the sources you use. Merely dumping them into your paper and summarizing them will not earn you a high score. Remember that you are in charge of the sources. You should consider yourself intellectually equal to the sources the exam provides. Thus, rather than deferring to their wisdom, you can choose to either agree or disagree with them. Typically, not all the sources will agree with one another. For those sources that contradict your position, you might concede and then refute their arguments.

The same points about engaging the quotations, rather than dumping them into your essay, hold true for the rhetorical analysis essay. However, in this essay, you should follow the quotation with an analysis of the strategy used and the effect it creates. Unlike the synthesis essay, because analysis **must always** follow the quotation, you don't have to work as hard to think about how to engage the text. You must analyze it.

Use Quotations Sparingly

An over-reliance on quotations means that you have moved into the category of information compiler and out of the category of writer. A patchwork of quotations stuck together with your words will not earn you a high score.

Don't Dump Quotations into Paragraphs

Background or context and/or the author or source from which the quotation is taken must be included near the quotation. Furthermore, the quotation must fit seamlessly into your paragraph.

> **Example** Source A makes the claim that "animals should not be used for experimental purposes." (Note: Here, the writer has not included a source citation because the source is indicated in the sentence.)
>
> **Example** Many scientists refuse to use animals for experimentation. One reason they feel this way is due to their beliefs that human beings should not exploit animals: "Though we can overpower animals and capture, cage, and drug them, we still have no right to use them for our own purposes" (Source A).

Keeping in mind what your thesis is arguing and the topic of the paragraph, you should use your own words to help explain it. In most cases, avoid beginning or ending a paragraph with a quotation.

Quote Accurately

The AP reader will be intimately familiar with the passage and will know when a line is misquoted. Such incorrectly cited quotations will cost you points.

Citation Verbs

Following is a handy list of verbs you might use to introduce or follow quotations.

- argues
- reveals
- claims
- emphasizes
- underscores
- indicates
- points out
- suggests
- recommends
- advises
- proposes
- concludes
- asserts
- speculates
- implies
- believes

THE BIG PICTURE: HOW TO PREPARE YEAR-ROUND

The AP Language and Composition Exam may be months away, but the time to start preparing is now. This section will help you to get the head start you need to make the most of your class and study time. When the night before the exam arrives, all you'll need is a quick review to be ready to earn a top score on the exam.

Below are some pointers to help keep you on track in the coming months.

- Set your goals—What score do you need, and what are your obstacles to achieving it?

- Practice your vocabulary—Study unfamiliar words and literary terms regularly.

- Read, read, read—Read challenging materials, including articles in newspapers and magazines.

- Write, write, write—Write your opinions and analyze the world around you.

- Follow a routine—take good notes in class, review them, and continue your work outside of class.

Use these strategies as you prepare throughout the year. As the exam gets closer, begin working through the review materials and test-taking strategies in the "Comprehensive Strategies and Review" section earlier in this book. When you are just a few days out, go back to the "Last-Minute Study Guide," section, do a final review of the key concepts, and make sure you have everything you need for exam day. You're ready to go!

Setting Your Goals

It would be great to live in a world where everyone got a 5 on all their AP tests. In this world, you would take every AP test under the sun, participate in every extracurricular activity available, and have plenty of time for after-school jobs, hanging out with friends, and whatever else you wanted to do. Since we do not live in that world, it's important to set realistic but ambitious goals and find ways to achieve them.

What Score Do You Need?

You want a 5, of course. If you're going into the exam planning to settle for less than that, adjust your attitude. Get more aggressive. Go for it.

That said, it's helpful to know how scores less than 5 can affect your future. If you are taking the exam in your senior year, check the policies of the schools you are considering attending. Many schools give credit for scores of 3 and above. By the time you get your scores, you should know what college you are attending, so your score will not affect your application. There's no harm in taking as many AP exams as you can.

What if your college application process is still a year or more away? When it comes to college admissions, nobody can tell for sure that this or that score on the AP exam will get you into College H or University P. The college admissions process is far too complicated to boil down to a few test scores. Students with straight-A records, 800 SAT scores, and

5s on their APs get waitlisted or outright rejected. Other students are admitted to their wildest reaches.

When a college admission committee considers your application, they're looking at the whole package: grades, test scores, athletics, extracurricular activities, community involvement, your essays, teacher recommendations, your passions, and special talents. So when you look at your record, think about how this AP score will work with the rest of the package. Did you write an essay about your love of writing, or are you applying to the liberal arts program? If so, the admissions committee might be looking for a 4 or a 5. On the other hand, if you're headed for the school of engineering, taking AP English may be seen as a sign of an ambitious and motivated student, and a 3 will seem quite respectable.

In the end, of course you want a 5. You always want to do the very best you can. Work for a 5. Study for a 5. Max your score. If the scores come back and you breathe a sigh of relief at your 3, that's fine, and no one has to know but you.

Which Tests Should You Take?

High school can be a juggling act. Between your challenging classes, extracurricular activities, and the many distractions available outside of school, many students wind up sleep deprived and, perhaps, wondering just why they signed up for so much punishment at the beginning of the year. If that describes you, take a realistic look at your schedule for the coming year. If you know which college you'll be attending, find out which AP exams can earn you college credit. Prioritize those that you think you'll have the best shot at, and those that can earn you credit.

If you're not taking an AP English class, you can still take the exam and do well. Many students earn high scores by studying on their own. If you have an aptitude for writing and know your way around a nonfiction passage, you should be in position for a successful exam. Just take a practice test to get an idea of what you're in for, follow the advice in this section, and use the rest of the book to help you prepare for the exam. If you are still applying to colleges, they will be impressed by your ambition, and if you're graduating this year, you'll be glad to be ahead of the game if you can earn college credit.

Don't Confuse the Two AP English Tests!

Don't forget that AP offers two English tests—the English Language and Composition exam and the AP English Literature exam. Make sure that you sign up for and show up for the correct exam. Unless you are preparing for both exams simultaneously, you will not be ready for the Literature exam. This exam tests knowledge and abilities that relate to literary works, like poetry and literature. The Language and Composition exam tests your ability to read and write about nonfiction works. Many a student has mistakenly signed up for the wrong exam, wasting countless hours of study.

Deciding Not to Take the Test

It's common to worry about receiving a low score on an AP exam, and tempting to skip it altogether. Maybe your nerves have temporarily gotten the better of you or you may feel inadequately prepared. Take a deep breath and think again. Aside from the registration fee, you don't have much to lose.

If you are worried about your score, don't be. Admissions officers are more likely to be impressed that you took the test than they are to penalize you for a low score. And, especially if you took AP English, a low score is better than no score. If you're in your senior year and know which college you'll be attending, you really have nothing to lose, except for the college credit you might earn by taking the test.

If you're lacking in confidence, don't underestimate what you know. You do not have to be able to answer every question accurately to earn a respectable score on the multiple-choice section. If you're a good writer, then you should be able to perform well on the essays. Unlike many AP exams, the English Language exam is a skills-based exam, which means that it's more of a test of how well you do something than a test of what you know. Being able to form a coherent, well-reasoned argument is more than half the battle in the essays. You don't have to memorize a formula or stuff your head with knowledge—just write persuasively, and you'll be fine.

If you choose not to take the exam, you might be left wondering what might have happened if you had taken it. Unanswered questions from our past come back to haunt us in the future! Go for it. Trust yourself and your abilities. Little is gained without risk.

Practicing Your Skills

If you're serious about getting a 5 on the AP Language and Composition Exam, your work should extend beyond the classroom. There are many ways (some of which are not even very painful!) to make preparing for the exam a way of life. What's more, these strategies will not only help you do well on the exam, they will give you a leg up in future classes and in life in general.

Practice Your Writing

The more you write, the better you will be. One good way to get motivated about writing is to write about topics that interest you. Perhaps you can start a blog where you write about interesting issues and ideas. You might also try your hand at writing for the school paper. Whatever the medium, try writing things that make a point and persuade your audience. Focus on writing as clearly and convincingly as you can—and be sure to back up your arguments with evidence. You'll be doing just these things when you write the essays in the AP exam.

Make the best use of your teacher and classwork as well. If your writing skills need work, meet with your teacher to improve. Rewrite your essays if you are given the option to do so. Jot down the problems that continually crop up in your writing and be sure to focus on them every time you are assigned a paper. Draft and redraft your essays. The more you practice writing, the better your writing will become. Even if the papers assigned have nothing to do with what is asked in the essay section of the exam, good writing is good writing.

If your grammar needs work, cast your eyes over a writing and grammar handbook. One particularly helpful choice is *The Hodges Harbrace Handbook*, a clearly written and easy-to-understand guide. There are many such grammar and writing books on the market. Go to your local bookstore and look around for the one that you most like.

Practice Your Vocabulary

Vocabulary can be helpful in both the multiple choice and essay sections. To help beef up your repertoire, you might purchase a vocabulary-enhancing workbook and work your way through it. Another good strategy is to make flashcards for SAT vocabulary words as well as rhetorical devices and strategies. Carry them around with you during the day and review them when you get the opportunity. You will be surprised to see how many words you learn just by flipping through the flashcards whenever possible.

If that seems overwhelming, commit to learning 10–15 words a week. Take an interest in the words you encounter in your assigned reading that you do not know. Look them up in a dictionary and be sure to write their definitions down. The mere act of writing the word and its definition will help to get the word in your head.

Read, Read, Read

Read a good newspaper, magazine, or news site for its news, analysis, and opinion articles. This will prepare you in two ways. First, knowledge of current events will be helpful for the persuasive essay, where you must draw on your own knowledge. Second, opinion articles and essays can help you read critically and analyze rhetorical strategies. Look at how the author is making his or her argument. See if you can identify the rhetorical strategies used and the types of appeals made.

Finally, look also at images such as charts, ads, and political cartoons, and analyze the information provided and the persuasive techniques used. This will be helpful in analyzing the visual in the synthesis essay.

Following a Routine

If you have months to go before the AP exam, the best way to maximize your time is to set a routine and form good habits. That means making the most of your time both in class and on your own.

Classroom Strategies

In class, take good notes. Keep your papers and organize them with the notes you have taken. Be sure to ask your teacher to clarify anything that you do not understand. Your teacher can be one of your best resources for ensuring that you do well on the exam. Even if you are not in an AP class, your teacher may be able to help you. Ask for pointers about the exam.

Take note of what your class is teaching to be sure it is preparing you for the exam. Is your class introducing you to the types of multiple-choice questions you will face? Is your class discussing the types of essays you will encounter and how to address them? Has the visual been discussed? If the answer to any of these questions is "no," you will need to study the materials required for the exam on your own. Fortunately, these materials are included in this book.

Outside Class

Make the most of your time outside class. Set aside time each week to practice your reading, writing, and vocabulary skills. In addition, take as many practice tests as you can. Review the answers and get extra practice in your areas of weakness. You can also visit the College Board web site and find the last several years' worth of essay prompts.

Take the practice test provided in this book and online. You can find the online practice test by visiting www.mymaxscore.com/aptests. Read the answers and explanations to the multiple-choice sections. Draft responses to the essay questions and judge them against the responses provided as well as the score guide. Finally, use some of the resources listed as follows for extra support.

Resources for Further Study

Books

Barron's *AP English and Language Composition* provides a thorough review that sticks to the AP test material. This is one of the better AP Language and Composition guidebooks on the market. Its practice tests are challenging. The chapter entitled "Getting Acquainted with the Test" is particularly useful for its passage annotations.

The Princeton Review's *Cracking the AP Language and Composition Exam* contains interesting synthesis questions and sources and useful responses. The multiple-choice tests are thoughtful and provide useful practice.

McGraw-Hill's *5 Steps to a 5* can be helpful. They, too, have useful annotations on passages and provide good practice synthesis questions.

Online

www.mymaxscore.com/aptests—At this site, you can take another free AP practice test. Detailed answers and explanations are provided for both the multiple-choice and essay sections.

www.collegeboard.com/student/testing/ap/sub_englang.html—At the College Board site, you can find sample tests, advice and general information about the exam. You'll find it particularly useful to review the last several years' worth of essay prompts, which are provided free on the site. Full tests are available for sale.

majortests.com/sat/wordlist.php—This is just one of many useful SAT word lists you can find online. If you have a long time to study, print out a list of the top 500 words and review it regularly to improve your vocabulary.

This book contains one practice test. Visit mymaxscore.com to download your free second practice test with answers and explanations.

AP English Language and Composition Practice Test

Three hours are allotted for this examination: one hour for Section I, which consists of multiple-choice questions; and two hours for Section II, which consists of essay questions. Section I is printed in this examination booklet. Section II is printed in a separate booklet.

SECTION I

TIME: 1 HOUR

NUMBER OF QUESTIONS: 52

PERCENT OF TOTAL GRADE: 45

Section I of this examination contains 52 multiple-choice questions. Select the choice that best answers each question. There is no penalty for guessing.

Use your time effectively, working as rapidly as you can without losing accuracy. Do not spend too much time on questions that are too difficult. Go on to other questions and come back to the difficult ones later if you have time.

<u>Directions:</u> This part includes selections from prose works and questions on their content, form, and style. After reading each passage, choose the best answer to each question.

Questions 1–10. Read the following passage carefully before you choose your answers.

The passage below is by Michel-Guillaume-Jean de Crevecoeur, a Frenchman who visited America during the 1700s.

In this great American asylum, the poor of Europe have by some means met together and in consequence of various causes; to what purpose should they ask one another what countrymen they are? Alas, two-thirds of them had no country. Can a wretch who wanders about, who
5 works and starves, whose life is a continual scene of sore affliction or pinching penury, can that man call England or any other kingdom his country? A country that had no bread for him, whose fields procured no harvest, who met with nothing but frowns of the rich, the severity of the law, with jails and punishments; who owned not a single foot of the
10 extensive surface of this planet? No! urged by a variety of motives, here they came. Everything has tended to regenerate them: new laws, a mode of living, a new social system; here they are become men; in Europe they were as so many useless plants, wanting vegetative mold and refreshing showers; they withered and were mowed down by want, hunger, and
15 war; but now by the power of transplantation, like all other plants they have taken root and flourished! Formerly they were not numbered in any civil lists of their country, except in those of the poor; here they rank as citizens. By what invisible power has this surprising metamorphosis been performed? By that of the laws and that of their industry. The laws,
20 the indulgent laws, protect them as they arrive, stamping on them the symbol of adoption; they receive ample rewards for their labors; these accumulated rewards procure them lands; those lands confer on them the title of freemen, and to that title every benefit is affixed which men

can possibly require. This is the great operation daily performed by our
25 laws. From whence proceed these laws? From our government. Whence
the government? It is derived from the original genius and strong desire
of the people ratified and confirmed by the crown. This is the great
chain which links us all; this is the picture which every province exhibits. Nova Scotia excepted. There the crown has done all; either there
30 were no people who had genius, or it was not much attended to; the
consequence is, that the province is very thinly inhabited indeed; the
power of the crown in conjunction with the musketos has prevented
men from settling there. Yet some parts of it flourished once, and it
contained a mild harmless set of people. But for the fault of a few lead-
35 ers, the whole was banished. The greatest political error the crown ever
committed in America was to cut off men from a country which wanted
nothing but men!

What attachment can a poor European emigrant have for a country
where he had nothing? The knowledge of the language, the love of
40 a few kindred as poor as himself, were the only cords that tied him;
his country is now that which gives him land, bread, protection and
consequence; *Ubi panis ibi patria*,[1] is the motto of all emigrants. What
then is the American, this new man? He is either an European, or the
descendent of an European, hence the strange mixture of blood, which
45 you will find in no other country. I could point out to you a family
whose grandfather was an Englishman, whose wife was Dutch, whose
son married a French woman, and whose present four sons have now
wives of different nations. He is an American, who leaving behind him
all ancient prejudices and manners, receives new ones from the new
50 mode of life he has embraced, the new government he obeys and the
new rank he holds.

He becomes an American by being received in the broad lap of our
great *Alma Mater.* Here individuals of all nations are melted into a
new race of men, whose labours and posterity will one day cause great

---

1   Where there is bread, there is my homeland.

55 changes in the world. Americans are the western pilgrims, who are car-
rying along with them that great mass of arts, sciences, vigor, and industry which began long since in the east; they will finish the great circle.
The Americans were once scattered all over Europe; here they are incorporated into one of the finest systems of population which has ever
60 appeared, and which will hereafter become distinct by the power of the
different climates they inhabit. The American ought therefore to love
this country much better than that wherein either he or his forefathers
were born.

1. The first paragraph proceeds primarily by

    A.   chronicling the successes of immigrants
    B.   cataloguing the effects of European injustices
    C.   juxtaposing American life to European life
    D.   discussing the immigration process
    E.   detailing the opportunities in America

2. What is the speaker's attitude toward America?

    A.   laudatory
    B.   objective
    C.   patronizing
    D.   reverent
    E.   naïve

3. The simile in lines 15–16 serves to emphasize the speaker's

    A.   contempt for that which is harmful to men
    B.   definition of what is needed for a man to be a man
    C.   desire to forge a new relationship with the earth
    D.   acceptance of poverty as destiny
    E.   acknowledgment of life lived with purpose

4. In the context of the simile in lines 13–16, the best interpretation of European men "as so many useless plants, wanting vegetative mold and refreshing showers..." (ll. 3–14) is that the European environment is

    A. barren
    B. stultifying
    C. fecund
    D. uninhabited
    E. poisonous

5. The speaker refers to a metamorphosis in line 18. Whom does he see as being *ultimately* responsible for this?

    A. the immigrant's own hard work
    B. the justice of American laws
    C. the people of America
    D. the support of the British monarchy
    E. the obtainment of land

6. In line 29 and following, the speaker discusses Nova Scotia. His tone in this section is best described as

    A. mean-spirited and dismissive
    B. cynical yet sympathetic
    C. reproachful yet forgiving
    D. dismayed and indignant
    E. reflective and condemning

7. The use of the simple sentence "Novia Scotia excepted" in line 29 signals

    I.   new points regarding why Nova Scotia failed to flourish
    II.   a contrast to the discussion which culminates in the phrase "this is the great chain that links us all"(ll. 27–28)
    III. a polemic that contrasts Americans to Nova Scotians
    A.   I only
    B.   II only
    C.   III only
    D.   I and II only
    E.   I, II, and III

8. Paragraph 2 contains all of the following rhetorical devices except

    A.   metonymy
    B.   cataloguing
    C.   metaphor
    D.   a loose sentence
    E.   oxymoron

9. What is the purpose of the sentence that begins on line 53: "Here individuals of all nations are melted into a new race of men, whose labours and posterity will one day cause great changes in the world"?

    A.   to qualify the author's thesis as implied in paragraph 1
    B.   to expand a point made in paragraph 2
    C.   to make a new point regarding what an American is
    D.   to signal a shift in tone
    E.   to acknowledge and refute a counter-argument

10. The last paragraph reveals the speaker's

    A.   tendency to exaggerate
    B.   desire to improve the lives of Americans
    C.   misguided optimism
    D.   denigration of all that is British
    E.   celebration of the future of Americans

Questions 11–27. Read the following passage carefully before you choose your answers.

The following passage is an excerpt from *The Crisis*, written by Thomas Paine in 1776, during the American Revolutionary War. In this excerpt, Paine argues for independence from England and for a self-governing America.

These are the times that try men's souls. The summer soldier and the sunshine patriot will, in this crisis, shrink from the service of their country; but he that stands it *now* deserves the love and thanks of man and woman. Tyranny, like hell, is not easily conquered; yet we have this

5 consolation with us, that the harder the conflict, the more glorious the triumph. What we obtain too cheap, we esteem too lightly; it is dearness only that gives everything its value. Heaven knows how to put a proper price upon its goods, and it would be strange indeed if so celestial an article as freedom should not be highly rated. Britain, with an army to

10 enforce her tyranny, has declared that she has a right not only to tax, but "to bind us in all cases whatsoever"; and if being bound in that manner is not slavery, then is there not such a thing as slavery, upon earth. Even the expression is impious, for so unlimited a power can belong only to God…

I have as little superstition in me as any man living, but my secret

15 opinion has ever been, and still is, that God Almighty will not give up a people to military destruction, or leave them unsupportedly to perish, who have so earnestly and so repeatedly sought to avoid the calamities of war, by every decent method which wisdom could invent. Neither have I so much of the infidel in me as to suppose that He has relinquished the

20 government of the world, and given us up to the care of devils; and as I do not, I cannot see on what grounds the King of Britain can look up to heaven for help against us: a common murderer, a highwayman, or a housebreaker has as good a pretense as he . . .

I once felt all that kind of anger which a man ought to feel against

25 the mean principles that are held by the Tories. A noted one, who kept

a tavern at Amboy, was standing at his door, with as pretty a child in his hand, about eight or nine years old, as I ever saw, and after speaking his mind as freely as he though was prudent, finished with this unfatherly expression, "Well! give me peace in my day." Not a man lives
30 on the continent, but fully believes that a separation must some time or other finally take place, and a generous parent should have said, "If there must be trouble, let it be in my day, that my children may have peace"; and this single reflection, well applied, is sufficient to awaken every man to duty. Not a place upon earth might be so happy
35 as America. Her situation is remote from all the wrangling world, and she has nothing to do but to trade with them. A man can distinguish himself between temper and principle, and I am as confident as I am that God governs the world, that American will never be happy till she gets clear of foreign dominion. Wars, without ceasing, will break out
40 till that period arrives, and the continent must in the end be conqueror; for though the flame of liberty may sometimes cease to shine, the coal can never expire . . . .

The heart that feels not now is dead; the blood of his children will curse his cowardice who shrinks back at a time when a little might have
45 saved the whole, and made *them* happy. I love the man that can smile in trouble, that can gather strength from distress, and grow brave by reflection. 'Tis the business of little minds to shrink; but he whose heart is firm, and whose conscience approves his conduct, will pursue his principles unto death. My own line of reasoning is to myself as straight and
50 clear as a ray of light. Not all the treasures of the world, so far as I believe, could have induced me to support an offensive war, for I think it murder; but if a thief breaks into my house, burns and destroys my property, and kills or threatens to kill me, or those that are in it, and to "bind me in all cases whatsoever" to his absolute will, am I to suffer it? What
55 signifies it to me whether he who does it is a king or a common man; my countryman or not my countryman; whether it be done by an individual villain, or an army of them? If we reason to the root of things we shall find no difference; neither can any just cause be assigned why we should

punish in the one case and pardon in the other. Let them call me rebel
60 and welcome, I feel no concern from it; but I should suffer the misery of
devils, were I to make a whore of my soul by swearing allegiance to one
whose character is that of a sottish, stupid, stubborn, worthless, brutish
man. I conceive likewise a horrid idea in receiving mercy from a being,
who at the last day shall be shrieking to the rocks and mountains to cover
65 him, and fleeing with terror from the orphan, the widow, and the slain
of America.

11. The dominant rhetorical mode that the author uses can best be clas-
sified as

    A. explanation

    B. description

    C. narration

    D. comparison

    E. persuasion

12. The author's purpose in the first paragraph is most likely

    A. to compare concrete reality to heavenly worth

    B. to establish the goodness of God and the American people

    C. to name the tension between the British and American governments

    D. to exhort the American people to look to heaven for help

    E. to identify God's power and Britain's weakness

13. In context, "summer soldier and the sunshine patriot" (ll. 1–2) is

    A. a simile for the American army's reserve soldiers

    B. an analogy for those citizen who are infidels

    C. synechdoche for the British soldiers stationed in America

    D. a metaphor for those who support the revolution only when convenient

    E. hyperbole for the government's specialized forces

14. In context, "dearness" (l. 6) implies

    A. affection
    B. thoughtfulness
    C. helplessness
    D. costliness
    E. money

15. According to the author, freedom (l. 9) is

    A. that which will vanquish cowards
    B. one of the most valuable commodities in heaven
    C. that which can be achieved quickly
    D. desirable but never attainable
    E. an issue only governments should negotiate

16. The "God" that the author refers to in l. 15 can be characterized as

    A. principled
    B. vengeful
    C. indifferent
    D. contemplative
    E. wrathful

17. Paine juxtaposes "superstition" (l. 14) with "infidel" (l. 19) to underscore his belief that

    A. in denying America freedom, Britain has squandered God's love
    B. in ignoring America's attempt to avoid war, Britain cannot hope for God's support
    C. in refusing to recognize America's moral superiority, Britain has sinned
    D. in repudiating God, Britain cannot understand America's desire for freedom
    E. in acknowledging America's independence, Britain would gain God's allegiance

18. The statement "If there must be trouble, let it be in my day, that my children may have peace" (ll. 32–33)

    A.   establishes Paine's empathy; all parents want their children to have lives of tranquility

    B.   underscores Paine's credibility; like all parents, he cares about the welfare of children

    C.   evokes ethos; Paine would rather have war in his time so that his and all children can enjoy a future without conflict

    D.   elicits logos; Paine is a rational parent who understands the needs of children

    E.   creates a tension between the adult need for war and the childhood need for calm

19. All of the following are aphorisms **except**

    A.   "Tyranny, like hell, is not easily conquered" (l. 4)

    B.   "the harder the conflict, the more glorious the triumph" (ll. 5–6)

    C.   "What we obtain too cheap, we esteem too lightly" (l. 6)

    D.   "not a place upon earth might be so happy as America" (ll. 34–35)

    E.   "though the flame of liberty may sometimes cease to shine, the coal can never expire" (ll. 41–42)

20. In lines 34–42, Paine feels that, in an ideal world, America's role in relation to the rest of the world would be

    A.   only one of commerce

    B.   one of aggressive self-assertion

    C.   more exalted than Britain's

    D.   one of world leadership

    E.   one of complete isolationism

21. The statement "The heart that feels not now is dead" (l. 43) is meant to

    I.   encourage revolutionary feeling through analogy
    II. elicit fearful concern by comparison
    III. inspire an emotional response through the use of synecdoche
    A.   I only
    B.   I and II only
    C.   II only
    D.   I and III only
    E.   III only

22. All of the following rhetorical devices are used in the last paragraph of the essay EXCEPT

    A.   aphorism
    B.   rhetorical question
    C.   polysyndeton
    D.   parallel construction
    E.   analogy

23. Paine uses asyndeton in lines 62–63 to

    A.   emphasize each of the problematic qualities of the king
    B.   underscore the incompetence and cruelty of the king
    C.   reveal the specific reasons why the king should be hated
    D.   analyze the character of the king
    E.   establish why the king should be distrusted

24. The central contrast in lines 59–63 is between

    A.   the judgment of others and personal integrity
    B.   name-calling and individual action
    C.   self-righteousness and indignation
    D.   criticism and individual worth
    E.   public perception and personal insight

25. The statement in lines 63–66, "I conceive likewise...slain of America," is a

    A. mythical analogy

    B. religious allusion

    C. literary reference

    D. metaphorical situation

    E. hyperbolic statement

26. The author's rhetorical style relies most on the use of

    A. allegory and pedantic rhetoric

    B. aphorism and emotional appeal

    C. symbolism and biblical allusion

    D. paradox and anecdote

    E. historical background and illustration

27. The overall tone of the essay is best described as

    A. pessimistic

    B. didactic

    C. urgent

    D. satirical

    E. optimistic

Questions 28–39. Read the following passage carefully before you choose your answers.

The following is an excerpt from Benjamin Franklin's autobiography.

It was about this time I conceiv'd the bold and arduous project of arriving at moral perfection. I wish'd to live without committing any fault at any time; I would conquer all that either natural inclination, custom, or company might lead me into. As I knew, or thought I knew,
5 what was right and wrong, I did not see why I might not always do the one and avoid the other. But I soon found I had undertaken a task of

more difficulty than I had imagined. While my care was employ'd in
guarding against one fault, I was often surprised by another; habit took
the advantage of inattention; inclination was sometimes too strong for
10   reason. I concluded, at length, that the mere speculative conviction that
it was our interest to be completely virtuous, was not sufficient to pre-
vent our slipping; and that the contrary habits must be broken, and good
ones acquired and established, before we can have any dependence on a
steady, uniform rectitude of conduct. For this purpose I therefore con-
15   trived the following method...

My intention being to acquire the *Habitude* of all virtues. I judg'd it
would be well not to distract my attention by attempting the whole at
once, but to fix on one at a time, and when I should be Master of that,
then to proceed to another, and so on till I should have gone thro' the
20   thirteen. And as the previous acquisition of some might facilitate the
acquisition of certain others, I arrang'd them with that view...

I determined to give a week's strict attention to each of the virtues
successively. Thus, in the first week, my great guard was to avoid even
the least offence against Temperance, leaving the other virtues to their
25   ordinary chance, only marking every evening the faults of the day.
Thus, if in the first week I could keep my first line, marked T, clear
of spots, I suppos'd the habit of that virtue so much strengthen'd and
its opposite weaken'd, that I might venture extending my attention to
include the next, and for the following week keep both lines clear of
30   spots. Proceeding thus to the last, I could go thro' a course compleat
in thirteen weeks, and four courses in a year. And like him who, having a garden to weed, does not attempt to eradicate all the bad herbs
at once, which would exceed his reach and his strength, but works on
one of the beds at a time, and, having accomplish'd the first, proceeds
35   to a second, so I should have, I hoped, the encouraging pleasure of
seeing on my pages the progress I made in virtue, by clearing successively my lines of their spots, till in the end, by a number of courses, I
should be happy in viewing a clean book, after a thirteen weeks' daily
examination.

40   My scheme of ORDER gave me the most trouble; and I found that, tho' it might be practicable where a man's business was such as to leave him the disposition of his time, that of a journeyman printer, for instance, it was not possible to be exactly observed by a master, who must mix with the world, and often receive people of business at their own hours. Or-
45   der, too, with regard to places for things, papers, etc., I found extreamly difficult to acquire. I had not been early accustomed to it, and, having an exceeding good memory, I was not so sensible of the inconvenience attending want of method. This article, therefore, cost me so much pain-ful attention, and my faults in it vexed me so much, and I made so little
50   progress in amendment, and had such frequent relapses, that I was almost ready to give up the attempt, and content myself with a faulty character in that respect, like the man who, in buying an ax of a smith, my neigh-bour, desired to have the whole of its surface as bright as the edge. The smith consented to grind it bright for him if he would turn the wheel; he
55   turn'd, while the smith press'd the broad face of the ax hard and heavily on the stone, which made the turning of it very fatiguing. The man came every now and then from the wheel to see how the work went on, and at length would take his ax as it was, without farther grinding. "No," said the smith, "turn on, turn on; we shall have it bright by-and-by; as yet, it is only
60   speckled." "Yes," said the man, "but I think I like a speckled ax best." And I believe this may have been the case with many, who, having, for want of some such means as I employ'd, found the difficulty of obtaining good and breaking bad habits in other points of vice and virtue, have given up the struggle, and concluded that "a speckled ax was best"; for something,
65   that pretended to be reason, was every now and then suggesting to me that such extream nicety as I exacted of myself might be a kind of foppery in morals, which, if it were known, would make me ridiculous; that a perfect character might be attended with the inconvenience of being envied and hated; and that a benevolent man should allow a few faults in himself, to
70   keep his friends in countenance.

28. The author's narrative style is characterized by his

    I.   sincere tone
    II. elevated diction
    III. self-awareness
    A.   I only
    B.   II only
    C.   I and III only
    D.   II and III only
    E.   I, II and III

29. Paragraph 1 moves from

    A.   ingenuous optimism to realistic insight
    B.   self-aggrandizement to self-deprecation
    C.   studied resolution to astonished indecision
    D.   personal evaluation to personal celebration
    E.   ingenuous examination to intuitive prejudice

30. One implication of lines 16–21 is that

    A.   virtues are easy to master when one is focused
    B.   arranged virtues are easily acquired by those determined to succeed
    C.   the achievement of certain virtues helps the achievement of others
    D.   the ability to be virtuous requires habit of mind
    E.   proceeding linearly results in virtue procurement

31. The analogy in lines 31–35, "And like him who…to a second" reveals that the elimination of moral flaws requires all of the following EXCEPT

    A.   removing one at a time
    B.   systematic effort
    C.   constraint by what is possible
    D.   success with one before attempting the next
    E.   experience with gardening and weeding

32. In paragraph 3, the author discusses the difficulty he has with the virtue of order. Which of the following is NOT a reason he gives for this difficulty?

   A.   People of business schedule visits according to their own schedules.

   B.   Order is not necessarily needed if one has a good memory.

   C.   If the habit of order is not formed early, it is difficult to acquire.

   D.   Without a method, order is difficult to establish.

   E.   Order is difficult to establish if its absence is not missed.

33. In context, the word "sensible" (l. 47) means

   A.   reasonable

   B.   practiced

   C.   wise

   D.   conscious

   E.   rational

34. In context, the word "want" (l. 48) means

   A.   desire

   B.   lack

   C.   abundance

   D.   longing

   E.   need

35. Franklin's attitude in paragraph 3 can best be described as

   A.   angry yet hopeful

   B.   thwarted but resigned

   C.   irritated but accepting

   D.   self-critical yet disdainful

   E.   bothered yet good hearted

36. The author employs an analogy in paragraph 3 to

    A. concede his inability to achieve moral perfection
    B. rationalize his refusal to accept failure in terms of moral perfection
    C. support his decision to attain moral perfection
    D. justify his concession to moral imperfection
    E. enumerate his reasons for his moral imperfection

37. The juxtaposition of the smith to the man who desires to have the surface of his axe made "bright" (l. 53) implies that

    A. the help of others makes hard work easier
    B. continued hard work makes all possible
    C. a positive attitude results in success
    D. encouragement makes work seem less fatiguing
    E. flaws make objects more valuable

38. "Countenance" (l. 70) is closest in meaning to

    A. facial expression
    B. agreement
    C. self-control
    D. approval
    E. happiness

39. In lines 64–70, "for something, that pretended…to keep his friends in countenance," which of the following is NOT given as a reason not to pursue moral perfection?

    A. Moral perfection is a vain and self-involved pursuit.
    B. Moral perfection evokes jealousy and dislike in others.
    C. Moral imperfections can be a bond among companions.
    D. Moral perfection is not a logical pursuit.
    E. Moral perfection can be a misguided pursuit.

Questions 40–53. Read the following passage carefully before you choose your answers.

The following is an excerpt from Andrew Carnegie's *Gospel of Wealth*, first published in June 1889.

The problem of our age is the proper administration of wealth, so that the ties of brotherhood may still bind together the rich and poor in harmonious relationship. The conditions of human life have not only been changed, but revolutionized, within the past few hundred years. In
5 former days there was little difference between the dwelling, dress, food, and environment of the chief and those of his retainers. The Indians are to-day where civilized man then was. When visiting the Sioux, I was led to the wigwam of the chief. It was just like the others in external appearance, and even within the difference was trifling between it and
10 those of the poorest of his braves. The contrast between the palace of the millionaire and the cottage of the laborer with us to-day measures the change which has come with civilization.

   This change, however, is not to be deplored, but welcomed as highly beneficial. It is well, nay, essential for the progress of the race, that
15 the houses of some should be homes for all that is highest and best in literature and the arts, and for all the refinements of civilization, rather than that none should be so. Much better this great irregularity than universal squalor. Without wealth there can be no Mæcenas.[1] The "good old times" were not good old times. Neither master nor
20 servant was as well situated then as today. A relapse to old conditions would be disastrous to both—not the least so to him who serves—and would sweep away civilization with it. But whether the change be for

---

1   Gaius Cilnius Maecenas (70 BC–8 BC) was a confidant and political advisor to the first Emperor of Rome, as well as an important patron for the new generation of Augustan poets. During the reign of Augustus, Maecenas served as a quasi–culture minister to the Emperor. His name has become a byword for a wealthy, generous and enlightened patron of the arts.

good or ill, it is upon us, beyond our power to alter, and therefore to be accepted and made the best of. It is a waste of time to criticize the
25 inevitable.

It is easy to see how the change has come. One illustration will serve for almost every phase of the cause. In the manufacture of products we have the whole story. It applies to all combinations of human industry, as stimulated and enlarged by the inventions of this scientific age. Formerly
30 articles were manufactured at the domestic hearth or in small shops which formed part of the household. The master and his apprentices worked side by side, the latter living with the master, and therefore subject to the same conditions. When these apprentices rose to be masters, there was little or no change in their mode of life, and they, in turn, educated
35 succeeding apprentices in the same routine. There was, substantially, so-cial equality, and even political equality, for those engaged in industrial pursuits had then little or no political voice in the State.

The inevitable result of such a mode of manufacture was crude ar-ticles at high prices. To-day the world obtains commodities of excellent
40 quality at prices which even the generation preceding this would have deemed incredible. In the commercial world similar causes have pro-duced similar results, and the race is benefited thereby. The poor enjoy what the rich could not before afford. What were the luxuries have become the necessaries of life. The laborer has now more comforts than
45 the landlord had a few generations ago. The farmer has more luxuries than the landlord had, and is more richly clad and better housed. The landlord has books and pictures rarer, and appointments more artistic, than the King could then obtain.

The price we pay for this salutary change is, no doubt, great. We
50 assemble thousands of operatives in the factory, in the mine, and in the counting-house, of whom the employer can know little or nothing, and to whom the employer is little better than a myth. All intercourse between them is at an end. Rigid Castes are formed, and, as usual, mutual ignorance breeds mutual distrust. Each Caste is without sympa-
55 thy for the other, and ready to credit anything disparaging in regard to

it. Under the law of competition, the employer of thousands is forced into the strictest economies, among which the rates paid to labor figure prominently, and often there is friction between the employer and the employed, between capital and labor, between rich and poor. Human
60   society loses homogeneity.

40. The implied assumption in paragraph 1 is that

    A.   visiting the Sioux reveals much about economic differences

    B.   the rich and the poor have a common bond of humanity

    C.   in the past there was little difference between the chief and his advisors

    D.   today there is a difference between how the rich and the poor live

    E.   the conditions of human life have changed during the past few hundred years

41. Paragraph 1 contains which rhetorical device?

    A.   catalogue

    B.   oxymoron

    C.   personification

    D.   simile

    E.   analogy

42. The statement that the "Indians are today where civilized man then was" (ll. 6–7) is

    A.   a statement of the obvious

    B.   an example of irony

    C.   a commentary on civilization

    D.   a value judgment

    E.   a dubious testimonial

43. The last sentence of paragraph 1, "The contrast…with civilization," functions as

    A. a conclusion to the argument made in paragraph 1
    B. a contrast to the argument made in paragraph 1
    C. a justification of the argument made in paragraph 1
    D. additional evidence for the argument made in paragraph 1
    E. a rationale for the argument made in paragraph 1

44. "This change" (l. 13) is a reference to

    A. the problem of the administration of wealth (l. 1)
    B. the revolution seen in the conditions of human life (ll. 3–4)
    C. the "little difference between dwelling, dress…retainers" (ll. 5–6)
    D. the "trifling difference" between the chief and his poorest braves (l. 9)
    E. "the contrast between the palace of the millionaire and the cottage of the laborer" (ll. 10–11)

45. The author's comment, "much better this great irregularity than universal squalor" (ll. 17–18), is an example of

    A. inductive reasoning
    B. appeal to tradition
    C. bandwagon appeal
    D. either/or fallacy
    E. *ad hominem* attacks

46. The implication of the author's claim that "without wealth there can be no Maecenas" (l. 18) is that money creates those who are

    A. knowledgeable and supportive of the arts
    B. sound and trusted political advisors
    C. informed and insightful ministers of culture
    D. distinguished and wealthy patrons of poetry
    E. trustworthy and sincere confidants

47. The purpose of paragraph 2 is to provide

    A.   evidence for the assumptions made in paragraph 1

    B.   justification for the argument made in paragraph 1

    C.   a rationale for the author's political views

    D.   a defense of socioeconomic class differences

    E.   an explanation of the master-apprentice relationship

48. The first sentence in paragraph 4, "The inevitable...at high prices," is an example of

    A.   a paradox

    B.   an appeal to logos

    C.   an appeal to tradition

    D.   faulty causality

    E.   an analogy

49. In paragraph 4, which is not stated as the result of the ability to obtain commodities today at reasonable prices?

    A.   The poor and the wealthy are both happier today.

    B.   The lives of the poor have been improved.

    C.   The lives of the wealthy have been improved.

    D.   We view as essential what was once viewed as a luxury.

    E.   The wealthy have greater access to art and literature.

50. The meaning of the word "salutary" (l. 49) is

    A.   doubtful

    B.   useful

    C.   misguided

    D.   beneficial

    E.   required

51. In context, the use of the word "myth" (l. 52) is best interpreted as meaning that the employer is

    A.   a heroic person
    B.   a supernatural being
    C.   a person who is not present in daily life
    D.   a person whose existence is a reality
    E.   similar to the Greek god Zeus

52. The author blames the fact that the "employer...is forced into the strictest economies" (ll. 56–57) on the

    A.   "friction" between "capital and labor" (l. 59).
    B.   "rates paid to labor" (l. 57)
    C.   lack of sympathy each "caste" has for the other (l. 54)
    D.   "friction between the employer and employed" (ll. 58–59).
    E.   "law of competition" (l. 56)

END OF SECTION 1

SECTION II

TOTAL TIME: 2 HOURS

NUMBER OF QUESTIONS: 3

PERCENT OF TOTAL GRADE: 55

Each question counts as one-third of the total essay section score.

Question 1 Synthesis Essay	suggested time—40 minutes
Question 2 Essay	suggested time—40 minutes
Question 3 Essay	suggested time—40 minutes

There is an additional 15 minutes for reading sources at the beginning of Section II. Section II of this examination requires answers in essay form. If you finish any question before time is up, you may go on to the next question. If you finish the examination in less than the time allotted, you may go back and work on any essay question you want.

Write your essays with a pen, preferably in black or dark blue ink. Be sure to write clearly and legibly. Cross out any errors you make.

QUESTION 1

suggested reading time—15 minutes
suggested writing time—40 minutes

Directions: The following prompt is based on the accompanying seven sources. This question requires you to synthesize a variety of sources into a coherent and well-written essay. When you synthesize sources, you include them to develop your position and cite them accurately. *Your position should be central; the sources should support your position. Avoid merely summarizing or paraphrasing the sources.* Remember to cite both direct and indirect references to the sources.

INTRODUCTION

Though we continue to turn to public and academic libraries for free access to the variety of resources they offer, many states and universities have cut their funding. In addition, in light of Internet access to information and digitalized books, libraries are being forced to reevaluate their role as places in which books are purchased, collected, and organized by those professionals educated to do so: the librarians.

ASSIGNMENT

Read the following seven sources carefully, including the introductory information. Then synthesize information from at least three of the sources and incorporate it into a coherent, well-developed essay that defends, challenges, or qualifies the claim that in the digital age, it is appropriate for libraries to shrink or eliminate their book and print sources in an effort to optimize their space for digital and Web-based research.

- Source A (Mary A. Dempsey)

- Source B (David Abel)

- Source C (John D. Sutter)

- Source D (Scott Carlson)

- Source E (Thomas Mann)

- Source F (Jonathan Shaw)

- Source G (Ed Stein)

Source A

The following is an excerpt from a Web letter written by Mary A. Dempsey, Commissioner of the Chicago Public Library, in response to a story by a local online news source, "Are Libraries Necessary or a Waste of Tax Money?"

Anna Davlantes
Fox 32 News Chicago
WFLD – TV
205 N. Michigan Avenue
Chicago, Illinois 60601

Dear Ms. Davlantes:

I am astounded at the lack of understanding of public libraries that your Monday evening story, *Are Libraries Necessary, or a Waste of Tax Money?* revealed. Public libraries are more relevant and heavily used today than ever before, and public libraries are one of the better uses of the taxpayers' dollars. Let me speak about the Chicago Public Library, which serves 12 million visitors per year. No other cultural, educational, entertainment or athletic organization in Chicago can make that claim. Those 12 million visitors come to our libraries for free access to books, journals, research materials, online information and computers, reference assistance from trained librarians, early literacy programs, English as a second language assistance, job search assistance, after-school homework help from librarians and certified teachers, bestsellers in multiple formats (print, audio, downloadable and e-book), movies, music, author events, book clubs, story times, summer reading programs, financial literacy programs, or simply a place to learn, dream and reflect.

The Chicago Public Library, through its 74 locations, serves every neighborhood of our city, is open seven days per week at its three largest locations, six days per week at 71 branch libraries and 24/7 on its website, which is filled with online research collections, downloadable content, reference help, and access to vast arrays of the Library's holdings and information.

Last year, Chicagoans checked out nearly 10 million items from the Chicago Public Library's 74 locations and the majority of those items were books...Especially in times of economic downturn, smart people turn to the public library as their free resource for books, information and entertainment in multiple formats—print, online, in person.

The suggestion by one of your interviewees that people do not need or use libraries anymore because of the Internet is simply not true. The Internet is one of the many tools that people use to live productive lives, and that tool can be accessed for free, and with free training by our staff, at the public library.

Source B

The following is an excerpt from a regional newspaper about Cushing Academy, a New England preparatory school. The author of the excerpt is David Abel.

Cushing Academy has all the hallmarks of a New England prep school, with one exception.

This year, after having amassed a collection of more than 20,000 books, officials at the pristine campus about 90 minutes west of Boston have decided the 144-year-old school no longer needs a traditional library. The academy's administrators have decided to discard all their books and have given away half of what stocked their sprawling stacks— the classics, novels, poetry, biographies, tomes on every subject from the humanities to the sciences. The future, they believe, is digital.

"When I look at books, I see an outdated technology, like scrolls before books," said James Tracy, headmaster of Cushing and chief promoter of the bookless campus. "This isn't *Fahrenheit 451* [the 1953 Ray Bradbury novel in which books are banned]. We're not discouraging students from reading. We see this as a natural way to shape emerging trends and optimize technology."

Instead of a library, the academy is spending nearly $500,000 to create a "learning center," though that is only one of the names in contention for the new space. In place of the stacks, they are spending $42,000 on three large flat-screen TVs that will project data from the Internet and $20,000 on special laptop-friendly study carrels. Where the reference desk was, they are building a $50,000 coffee shop that will include a $12,000 cappuccino machine.

And to replace those old pulpy devices that have transmitted information since Johannes Gutenberg invented the printing press in the 1400s, they have spent $10,000 to buy eighteen electronic readers made by Amazon.com and Sony. Administrators plan to distribute the readers, which they're stocking with digital material, to students looking to spend more time with literature.

Those who don't have access to the electronic readers will be expected to do their research and peruse many assigned texts on their computers.

"Instead of a traditional library with 20,000 books, we're building a virtual library where students will have access to millions of books," said Tracy, whose office shelves remain lined with books. "We see this as a model for the 21st-century school."

Source C

The following is an excerpt from an article by John D. Sutter titled "Are Libraries Going Extinct?"

The move towards online education and web-based learning materials is leaving one very significant victim in its wake: campus libraries. For the last ten years or so, books have been slowly phased out of a college student's life and personal computers have been phased in. Increasingly, materials are available online both on the Internet and through online journal databases. When connected to the campus network, students are usually able to access the catalogue at the campus's main library from the comfort of their dorm room. Even dissertation research, which used to entail hours of sleepless nights roaming the stacks for journals, can now be done from home. What can campus libraries do to attract students, then, when their main commodity is not required? Are they in danger of becoming the dinosaurs on campus?

First of all, there are three groups of students who will never abandon the library. The first is the segment of the student body who enjoy roaming the stacks, finding old books and imagining the events these books have lived through. For these students, reading a digitized version holds no candle to actually touching a copy of Victor Hugo's *Les Miserables*. These students will always visit the library so there is no need to worry about them leaving. A second body of folks who aren't jumping ship are the students who study in the library coffee shop. They are there for the peace and quiet that is unachievable at Starbucks. As long as the coffee stays, they will be there typing and researching away on their own computers. The third group of students who will always visit the library are those who, in the final hours before a due date or exam, hope to cram in as much information as possible including that which may be available through osmosis. Being surrounded by important books and brilliant works as they study increases the potential for tidbits of information to seep their way into the mind.

However, there are all those other students on campus who may not even know where the library is. This is the target audience libraries should find a way to draw in for a visit. They should promote and advertise themselves the way that the campus bookstore does. They should have events like student musicians who play outside the library and opening night (with free pizza, of course) for their monthly materials exhibits. They should investigate using non-library activities as bait to lure students in and then let the card catalogue speak for itself. They should find a way to, as they did in the pre-digital world, make themselves a hub for student activity.

Libraries are a true treasure and cannot be replaced by the Internet. It's critical that they find a way to keep themselves as an active part of the campus community. This will require them to do something that libraries are not terribly familiar with: change.

Source D

The following is an excerpt from an article in an academic journal. The article, by Scott Carlson, is entitled "Do Libraries Really Need Books?" Marquette University is a Catholic, Jesuit university located in Milwaukee, Wisconsin.

The divergence between the book and the computer is realized in the design of Marquette's $47-million library project, a three-story skeleton of scaffolding and concrete that is rising next to the boxy Memorial Library, a relic from the 1950s.

The new library will hold a small collection of popular and recent books, along with reference material and part of the special collections. But most of the building will be devoted to multimedia stations and instruction rooms, computer labs, reading rooms, and group-study areas... Most of the university's 1.3 million books and print periodicals will be stored in old Memorial...

Some faculty members, however, wonder if the new library will give too much emphasis and attention to computers and other new technology, outshining the traditional print media. Lance R. Grahn, chairman of the history department, represented the faculty on the library's planning committee. He already sees many students limiting themselves to quick database searches, and he worries about how that reliance affects their education. "Too many students think that they can go to the Web, get their answer, and the learning is done," he says.

The doubts about the new library's emphasis also resonate with graduate students like Scott Celsor, a doctoral candidate in theology. "It concerns me that they are overemphasizing the role of technology in the future," he says while at work on a paper in one of Memorial's periodical rooms.

Mr. Burckel has doubts, too. The dean, a historian by training, has dug up some of the presumptuous things that futurists of old have said about technology and education, like the mid-20th-century prediction that all students would someday earn their degrees through television. "I'm enough of a historian not to be cynical about prognostication," he says, "but enough to know that prognosticators are not always accurately predicting." And he laughs about a recent interaction with a student who thought that a reference book was "the print version of the CD."

If students aren't checking out books, or aren't getting unrestricted, immediate access to books, they are missing out on a vital source of instruction, says…a reference librarian at the Library of Congress… He insists that as a medium for both storing and dispensing information, books rival, even surpass, their digital counterparts. "There is a real difference between information and knowledge, and between knowledge and understanding," he says. "I think the screen-display formats are biased toward information. People will tend toward easier things than more difficult things."

"Do Libraries Really Need Books?" by Scott Carlson (Copyright © 2002, The Chronicle of Higher Education. Reprinted with Permission.)

Source E

The following is an excerpt from a response to an article by Karen Calhoun. Calhoun's article was entitled "The Changing Nature of the Catalog and Its Integration with Other Discovery Tools." Calhoun's article was written for the Library of Congress.

The differences between scholarship and quick information seeking

Scholars, if I may be so bold as to draw on my own experience of working with thousands of them over a very long period, have these concerns that are not shared by quick "information seekers":

1) Scholars seek as clear and extensive an *overview* of *all* relevant sources as they can achieve.

2) They are especially concerned that they do not overlook sources that are unusually important, significant, or standard in their field of inquiry.

3) They do not wish to unnecessarily duplicate prior research.

4) They particularly wish to be aware of cross-disciplinary connections to their work.

5) They wish to find *current* books on a subject categorized with the *prior* books on the same subject, so that the newer works can be perceived in the context of the existing literature—not just in connection with the much smaller subset of titles that are currently in print. (Advanced scholars also wish for similar categorization of English language books with relevant foreign language titles, so that a worldwide context of literature on their subject can be easily discerned.)

6) They particularly appreciate mechanisms that enable them to *recognize* highly relevant sources whose *keywords they cannot think up in advance*....

7) Although they are more cognizant of the need for extended effort and the need to check multiple sources beyond the "first screen" of any Internet retrievals, they also wish to avoid having to sort through huge lists or displays—from any source—in which relevant materials are buried within inadequately sorted mountains of chaff having the "right" keywords in the wrong conceptual contexts.

Google-type "relevance ranked" keyword searching cannot solve these problems; in fact, it exacerbates all of them. It is not even particularly good for keyword searching, in comparison with other databases... Nor does Google-type searching allow searchers to limit the appearance of words to particular fields, because it does not distinguish or segregate such fields (title, contents, notes, bibliographies, etc.) to begin with. It just jumbles everything together. Although she does sometimes use the word "scholars," Calhoun does not use it in any way that clearly distinguishes its referent from quick "information seekers."

Source F

The following is an excerpt from *Harvard Magazine* entitled "Harvard's Libraries Deal with Disruptive Change," by Jonathan Shaw.

"People want information 'anytime, anyplace, anywhere,'" says Helen Shenton, the former head of collection care for the British Library who is now deputy director of the Harvard University Library. Users are changing—but so, too, are libraries. The future is clearly digital.

Yet if the format of the future is digital, the content remains data. And at its simplest, scholarship in any discipline is about gaining access to information and knowledge, says Peter Bol, Carswell professor of East Asian languages and civilizations. In fields such as botany or comparative zoology, researchers need historical examples of plant and animal life, so they build collections and cooperate with others who also have collections. "You need books. But in physics or chemistry, where the research horizon is constantly advancing, much of the knowledge created in the past has very little relevance to current understanding." In that case, [Carswell] says, "you want to be riding the crest of the tidal wave of information that is coming in right now. We all want access to information, and in some cases that will involve building collections; in others, it will mean renting access to information resources that will keep us current. In some cases, these services may be provided by a library, in others by a museum or even a website."

In advocating for the continued importance of books, and raising his concern that this could become the "lost decade" for acquisitions to Harvard's library collections, Hamburger [the Francke professor of German art and culture] emphasizes that he is not framing the University's current crisis in terms of books versus new media. "We need both, and we'll continue to need both. I think we have to take as a premise that the library is a vast, far-flung, varied institution, as varied and diverse as the intellectual community of the University itself, working for a range of constituents almost impossible to conceive of, and it's not just a service organization. I would even go so far as to call it the nervous system of our corporate body.... The greatness of this university in the past and in the future rests on the greatness of our library. Without the library—old, new, digital, printed—this institution wouldn't be what it is."

Copyright © 2010 Harvard Magazine Inc. Excerpted and reprinted, with permission, from Jonathan Shaw, "Gutenberg 2.0: Harvard's Libraries Deal with Disruptive Change," May-June 2010 (112:5, 36-41, 82f). All rights reserved.

Source G

Cartoon by Ed Stein

Cartoon from Stein Library (Ed Stein: copyright *Rocky Mountain News*/Dist. by United Feature Syndicate, Inc.)

> QUESTION 2
>
> (Suggested time—40 minutes. This question counts for one-third of the total essay section.)

The following is an excerpt from an essay by contemporary African American male author Brent Staples. Read the excerpt carefully, and then write an essay that analyzes what rhetorical strategies Staples uses to convey his view of what it means to be a African American man in society today.

My first victim was a woman—white, well-dressed, probably in her late twenties. I came upon her late one evening on a deserted street in Hyde Park, a relatively affluent neighborhood in an otherwise mean, impoverished section of Chicago. As I swung onto the avenue behind
5 her, there seemed to be a discreet, uninflammatory distance between us. Not so. She cast back a worried glance. To her, the youngish black man—a broad six feet two inches with a beard and billowing hair, both hands shoved into the pockets of a bulky military jacket—seemed menacingly close. After a few more quick glimpses, she picked up her pace
10 and was soon running in earnest. Within seconds, she disappeared into a cross street.

That was more than a decade ago. I was twenty-two years old, a graduate student newly arrived at the University of Chicago. It was in the echo of that terrified woman's footfalls that I first began to know the
15 unwieldy inheritance I'd come into—the ability to alter public space in ugly ways. It was clear that she thought herself the quarry of a mugger, a rapist, or worse. Suffering a bout of insomnia, however, I was stalking sleep, not defenseless wayfarers. As a softy who is scarcely able to take a knife to a raw chicken—let alone hold one to a person's throat—I
20 was surprised, embarrassed, and dismayed all at once. Her flight made me feel like an accomplice in tyranny. It also made it clear that I was indistinguishable from the muggers who occasionally seeped into the

area from the surrounding ghetto. That first encounter, and those that
followed, signified that a vast, unnerving gulf lay between nighttime
25 pedestrians—particularly women—and me. And I soon gathered that
being perceived as dangerous is a hazard in itself. I only needed to turn a
corner into a dicey situation, or crowd some frightened, armed person in
a foyer somewhere, or make an errant move after being pulled over by a
policeman. Where fear and weapons meet—and they often do in urban
30 America—there is always the possibility of death.

In that first year, my first away from my hometown, I was to become
thoroughly familiar with the language of fear. At dark, shadowy inter-
sections, I could cross in front of a car stopped at a traffic light and elicit
the thunk, thunk, thunk, thunk of the driver—black, white, male, or
35 female—hammering down the door locks. On less traveled streets after
dark, I grew accustomed to but never comfortable with people crossing
to the other side of the street rather than pass me. Then there were the
standard unpleasantries with policemen, doormen, bouncers, cabdrivers,
and others whose business it is to screen out troublesome individuals
40 before there is any nastiness.

I moved to New York nearly two years ago and I have remained an
avid nightwalker. In central Manhattan, the near-constant crowd cover
minimizes tense one-on-one street encounters. Elsewhere—in Soho, for
example, where sidewalks are narrow and tightly spaced buildings shut
45 out the sky—things can get very taut indeed.

After dark, on the warrenlike streets of Brooklyn where I live, I often
see women who fear the worst from me. They seem to have set their
faces on neutral, and with their purse straps strung across their chests
bandolier-style, they forge ahead as though bracing themselves against
50 being tackled. I understand, of course, that the danger they perceive is
not a hallucination. Women are particularly vulnerable to street violence, and young black males are drastically overrepresented among the
perpetrators of that violence. Yet these truths are no solace against the
kind of alienation that comes of being ever the suspect, a fearsome entity
55 with whom pedestrians avoid making eye contact...

Relatively speaking, however, I never fared as badly as another black male journalist. He went to nearby Waukegan, Illinois a couple of summers ago to work on a story about a murderer who was born there. Mistaking the reporter for the killer, police officers hauled him from his car

60 at gunpoint and but for his press credentials would probably have tried to book him. Black men trade tales like this all the time.

Over the years, I learned to smother the rage I felt at so often being taken for a criminal. Not to do so would surely have led to madness. I now take precautions to make myself less threatening. I move about

65 with care, particularly late in the evening. I give a wide berth to nervous people on subway platforms during the wee hours, particularly when I have exchanged business clothes for jeans.

And on late-evening constitutionals I employ what has proved to be an excellent tension-reducing measure: I whistle melodies from Beethoven

70 and Vivaldi and the more popular classical composers. Even steely New Yorkers hunching toward nighttime destinations seem to relax, and occasionally they even join in the tune. Virtually everybody seems to sense that a mugger wouldn't be warbling bright, sunny selections from Vivaldi's *Four Seasons*. It is my equivalent to the cowbell that hikers

75 wear when they know they are in bear country.

Essay reprinted with permission from the author. Brent Staples writes editorials on politics and culture for the *New York Times* and is the author of the memoir *Parallel Time*.

QUESTION 3

(Suggested time—40 minutes. This question counts for one-third of the total essay section.)

Erich Fromm wrote his essay "Disobedience as a Psychological and Moral Problem" immediately after the Cuban missile crisis, when people feared a third world war in which nuclear weapons would be launched, causing a nuclear holocaust.

At the end of his essay Fromm states, "Man [and woman] has lost the capacity to disobey, he is not even aware of the fact that he obeys. At this point in history, the capacity to doubt, to criticize, to disobey may be all that stands between a future for mankind and an end to civilization."

Write an essay in which you evaluate the pros and cons of Fromm's statement and then indicate why you find one position more persuasive than another. Support your argument with appropriate evidence from your reading, observation, or experience.

Answers and Explanations

Section I

Passage 1

1. **C.** The passage compares what life was like in England to what life is like in America. The effect of the juxtaposition reveals that by comparison, America is the better place to live for a variety of reasons. A and B cannot be correct because the injustices and successes are never described in isolation from each other. Answer E is incorrect because specific opportunities are not listed throughout the passage but only in particular places.

2. **A.** Knowing the meaning of words is key to the answer for this question. The speaker has nothing but praise for America. Answer choices B, C, and E can be dismissed almost immediately if the denotation of these words is known. Answer A is better than D because the speaker's tone is more excited than solemn.

3. **B.** The simile compares men to plants. In line 12, the speaker states, "here they are become men." The speaker then goes on to define what it means to be a man; a man must have "use" and "purpose." Usefulness and purpose can only occur in environment that is nurturing and therefore allows for this flourishing.

4. **A.** Again, much of the question rests on vocabulary knowledge. *Stultifying* means to render someone ineffectual or useless. The speaker's point has been that Britain treats its lower classes badly; they are punished harshly and deprived of a way to make a living. Answer B is an attractive choice but does not get at the meaning of the simile which goes beyond mere injustice. *Fecund* means fertile and therefore is wrong. *Barren* is merely a play on the simile itself without any real connection to what the simile is trying to reveal. *Poisonous* is too harsh; poison kills, whereas the poor live but suffer.

5. **D.** Lines 18–24 are a catalogue (list) of what the "invisible power" (l. 18) is comprised of. Lines 24–29 list the links that have created the

"great chain" named in lines 27–28. The final point the speaker makes is that all of his points are derived from "the crown" (l. 27). Answer C is an attractive answer, as the speaker states that government is "is derived from the original genius and strong desire of the people" (26–27). However, his sentence does not end with this point. The people may have this genius and power, but it is the crown that allows them to exercise them. Answers A and B are clearly wrong because there is no mention of what these answers state. Answer B is wrong because the justice of American laws is a result of the British monarchy's allowing these laws to exist.

6. **D.** The speaker's tone changes in this section. Before this section, the speaker has nothing but praise for America, and though he castigates Britain for its treatment of its people, he still supports the crown. In these lines the speaker is critical of the actions of the British leaders and condemns the crown for the first time stating it committed the "greatest political error" (l. 35) by not allowing Nova Scotia to be inhabited.

7. **D.** What follows the use of the simple sentence is a catalogue of the reasons why Nova Scotia did not "flourish" and how "the crown" is responsible for Nova Scotia's situation. Thus, I and II are both correct. Knowing that III is incorrect rests on your knowledge of the word *polemic* as well as your understanding of the essay itself. A polemic is a passionate argument against something or someone. Though the speaker criticizes the crown's actions in Nova Scotia, his words are not polemical. Further, there is no contrast between Americans and Nova Scotians in what follows the short sentence.

8. **E.** Identifying the correct answer lies in your knowledge of rhetorical terms and your ability to recognize their usage. Metonymy is seen in the use of the word "bread" (l. 41). Metonymy substitutes one term for another term closely associated with it. "Bread" implies all food or that which nourishes. "Cataloguing" is merely listing. Listing is seen in lines 46–48. In line 40, "cords that tied him" is a metaphor comparing what connects people to their country to ropes or "cords." The loose

sentence begins on line 48: "He is an American…" Loose sentences are sentences in which the main idea comes first and then is supported by what follows. "He is an American" is the main idea; what follows are what defines an American. There are no oxymorons, pairs of words that contradict each other, in this paragraph.

9. **C.** Though this sentence signals that new points about what being an American entails and promises, there is no tone shift. De Crevecoeur's tone regarding his view of America has remained the same throughout the passage; he has nothing but praise for America. There is no quali-fication of the first paragraph's thesis, as paragraph 1 is a discussion of what America offers versus what is experienced in Britain. No counter-argument to the speaker's claims about America exists in the passage as a whole.

10. **E.** This is a tricky question, because a quick reading could lead you to choose answer A. However, in some ways, America could become the "melting pot" that De Crevecoeur predicts. Thus, he describes a pos-sibility; possibilities are not exaggerations. De Crevecoeur is not seeking to improve the lives of Americans. Answer D is incorrect as there is no denigration of Britain in this paragraph. Answer C can also be elimi-nated almost immediately because though optimistic, there is nothing "misguided" about De Crevecoeur's optimism. If what he claims comes to pass, the world would be a better place. Thus, answer E is correct because the paragraph is about what the future of America could look like. The speaker's use of the word "hereafter" (l. 60) is a clue that E is the correct answer.

Passage 2

11. **E.** This question should be fairly easy because the introduction states that Paine *argues* for independences and self-governance. Argument tries to *persuade* listeners. The use of the word "dominant" in the stem de-notes that the question is asking you to identify the mode to which all

other lesser modes point. There is description and narration in the passage (see paragraph 2); however, these, too, are used to persuade. Paine also draws comparisons between the King and a murderer, a highwayman, and a housebreaker (ll. 22–23). However, here again, these comparisons are employed to persuade the reader that the King is misguided if not criminal in his intentions toward America.

12. **A.** This question requires that you look at the paragraph as a whole. By doing so, you can eliminate some answers quite easily. B should strike you as obviously incorrect. Paine makes no attempt at establishing any view of God or the American people. The only mention he makes of God is in line 13, and here it is a reference to God's omnipotence. In the first line of the paragraph, mention is made of difficult times; however, Paine does not overtly name the reasons for this difficulty. He merely moves to a comparison between the difficulty of overcoming tyranny to the difficulty of overcoming hell (l. 4). D is the most obviously incorrect answer. Paine's essay is about taking action and not relying on others for help. E is incorrect because although Paine claims God has "unlimited power" (l. 13), he does not identify Britain as weak. Instead, he points out why Britain is wrong to claim it has the right to "bind..." (l. 11) when in fact only God has the rights Britain claims for herself. Paine begins the paragraph with what is occurring in America, and America's desire for freedom. He then makes the point that freedom is a "celestial" article worth a great deal (ll. 8–9). *Celestial* means typical of heaven.

13. **D.** Know your rhetorical terms! This question requires that you understand not only meaning but also rhetorical devices. If you know your devices then you can eliminate all of the answers almost immediately. Similarly, if you are good at interpretation, you can do the same. If you are good at both, skip this explanation altogether and move on. Let's start with meaning created by word choice. Both *summer* and *sunshine* imply comfortable and pleasant weather. War is neither pleasant nor comfortable. Thus, the implication of Paine's diction should lead you

to a Answer D. The interpretation given in the other answers simply cannot be supported by Paine's word choice. Similes must use *like* or *as* in a comparison between two unlike objects. Like a simile, an analogy is a comparison between unlike things that share some point of similarity. No parallel is given. Synecdoche uses a part to stand in for the whole. There is no larger part to which *summer* or *sunshine* could refer. Finally, hyperbole is exaggeration. It should be evident that nothing is being exaggerated.

14. **D.** This is a question that forces you to rely on context clues. Line 6 uses the word *cheap*. Cheap implies low in cost or value. Lines 6–7 makes the connection between "dearness" and "value." Thus, you should be able to deduce that "dearness" is that which gives something value. Something that is costly is valuable. Thus, D is the answer. Answers A and C play on the connotations of the word "dear" when used as a term of endearment. These connotations do not make sense in the context of the passage. "Money" does not fit because money does not create value. Money is itself valuable.

15. **B.** This question echoes question 12. If you answered 12 correctly, then you should be able to answer this question correctly as well. As indicated in the answer to question 12, freedom is described as a "celestial article" (ll. 8–9). Again, *celestial* means belonging to or typical of heaven. None of the other answers engage this aspect of Paine's point about freedom and why it should be sought and valued.

16. **A.** Paine describes the colonists as having, by every means possible, sought to avoid war (ll. 17–18). He describes God as a being who would let those who have sought to avoid war go unsupported or allow them to be given up to "military destruction" (ll. 15–16). A God who supports and protects a worthy people is a "principled" God; "principled" implies "possessing moral characteristics." Eliminating the other choices is only a matter of vocabulary knowledge.

17. **B.** Paine uses *superstition* to establish his belief in a just God. He uses the word *infidel* to underscore his point that the God in whom he believes would never allow Britain to rule America, particularly since the King's behavior can be compared to that of a criminal. There is no discussion of God's love or freedom in this paragraph; thus, A is wrong. There is no mention of American moral superiority, as that would be considered hubristic. Paine wants to convince, not offend. Thus, C is wrong. *Repudiate* means to deny. Paine does not state that Britain denies God's existence; in fact, he states that they might misguidedly look to Heaven for support. D is therefore wrong. Finally, nothing in the paragraph indicates that God would become an ally of the King's if America were allowed to gain independence from Britain.

18. **C.** To answer this question correctly, you must understand not only vocabulary but also how various appeals are elicited. An appeal to ethos establishes the speaker's trustworthiness and moral integrity. Paine does this when he claims he would rather fight now so that future generations can live in peace. He has established the fact that he is concerned not only about his own children's welfare but also about the welfare of the children of all Americans. B is an attractive distracter. However, this answer misses the mark because it does not explain why the war must be fought immediately. Answer A can be eliminated because the war is not focused on creating tranquility. Answer D can be eliminated because the parent/child relationship is an emotional rather than a rational relationship. Logos is an appeal to reason and rational ideas. E is incorrect because there is no adult need for war just for war's sake.

19. **D.** An aphorism is a succinct statement that expresses a universal truth. Some examples of aphorisms are "Don't judge a book by its cover" and "An eye for an eye makes the whole world blind." Even if you do not know what an aphorism is, D stands out because it doesn't sound the same as the other choices. Answer D refers to a specific place, America, and the point it makes about America is not really

that deep. The other choices use abstract words to point to a large and profound truth.

20. **A.** This is a question that requires close reading. There is nothing tricky here. Line 36 states that America "has nothing to do but to trade with them." Because the author states that trade would be the only relationship maintained with the outside world (which would mean that America would not be completely isolationist), the other answers can easily be eliminated.

21. **E.** Again, this question requires that you know your rhetorical terms. The most attractive distracter is D; however, there is no analogy in the given statement. The use of synecdoche emphasizes the "heart" for the whole person. Hearts are where we tend to locate emotions.

22. **C.** Sound familiar? Know your rhetorical terms and be able to identify them. Aphorisms appear in lines 47–49. Rhetorical questions appear in lines 54–57. Parallel constructions appear in lines 45–46. An analogy appears in lines 52–54, ending with "suffer it?" Polysyndeton is the repeated use of conjunctions in a list. No list appears in this paragraph.

23. **B.** Asyndeton is the lack of conjunctions in a list. Paine has not included the conjunction "and" before the last adjective he uses to describe the king. The cumulative effect of Paine's adjectives running together is the emphasis of a dominant impression: the king is incompetent and cruel and therefore does not deserve the loyalty of the colonialists. Answer A can be eliminated almost immediately because, by definition, it is polysyndeton that emphasizes each individual item in a list. Answer C is an attractive distracter but can be discounted because Paine is not arguing that the king should be hated. He is arguing that "allegiance" (l. 61) should be withheld from a man who does not deserve it. The reasoning for the incorrectness of answer C holds true for answer E. D is incorrect because there is no analysis.

24. **A.** To choose the correct answer, you must be able to identify the contrast to which the lines point as well as understand the meaning of the lines. Paine states, "Let them call me a *rebel*...but I should suffer the miseries of devils were I to make a *whore* of my soul..." (ll. 59–61). Paine is willing to risk the label "rebel" by defying the king's desires. If Paine were to be called a "rebel," it would be because others are judging his actions as rebellious. We tend to think of *whore* as meaning a woman who sells sexual favors. However, in this case, Paine is using it to imply that for him, obedience to the king implies moral corruption akin to sexual debauchery. The archaic definition of *whore* is to corrupt or debauch in a moral sense. Paine's personal integrity is what stops him from swearing allegiance to the king. Answer B is attractive because the first half of the answer is accurate—"rebel" is name-calling; however, the second half of answer B is incorrect because no action is taken. Paine refuses to swear allegiance. Answers C and D can be dismissed because they do not engage the meaning of Paine's words as fully as do answer A and even answer B. Answer C is incorrect because "rebel" is a label applied by others; thus, there is no self to be self-righteous.

25. **B.** Many works of fiction and nonfiction use biblical and/or religious references to make a point. These references are called allusions. Thus, for those of us without a religious background, these references can seem obscure. For Christians, "Last day" is a reference to Judgment Day, the day on which God judges all of humanity. Paine's point is that on Judgment Day, the king will find himself hiding from the innocent he has killed, as they will judge him as evil.

26. **B.** This question requires that you consider the passage as a whole and identify the dominant style Paine employs. What appears to be a difficult question upon first read is actually simple; many of the answers include rhetorical strategies that Paine does not employ. There is no allegory in the passage. Allegory is tied to symbolism, and there is also no symbolism. Allegories are works that have a literal, but more importantly, a symbolic meaning. Paine is quite clear in what he says, why he

says it and what actions he hopes his comments will elicit. Though some of the stories he relates may be anecdotal, for example the story he tells of the Tory father in lines 24–29, he does not employ paradox—a seeming contradiction that is in fact true. Finally, Paine does not provide any historical background, as he is writing for the people of his time period.

27. **C.** If you answered question 1 correctly, then you should be able to answer this question correctly as well. Persuasion urges the listener to take action or to believe what the author/speaker argues. Answers A and E can be dismissed as incorrect because Paine is neither overly positive nor overly negative. *Didactic* implies moral instruction, often when not welcome. Answer D can be eliminated at first read because Paine is never satiric. A satire mocks a social institution to elicit change or point out flaws. No social institution is mocked; instead, the king and his actions are denigrated.

Passage 3

28. **C.** An autobiography is a narrative of the author's life. Narrative styles differ; however, in the excerpt given, Franklin is honest in his desire to attain moral perfection and critical of his inability to do so. He is quick to judge his faults and, at the end of his narrative, acknowledges the reasons why he gives up his pursuit of moral perfection. Some of the reasons he gives are less than flattering. Though we, as modern readers, may find his prose difficult to understand, his writing is straightforward and unaffected. Thus, C is the only correct answer.

29. **A.** It is naïve to believe that one can achieve moral perfection merely by eliminating faults and adopting virtues. However, such a pursuit does entail a positive view of one's capabilities. By the paragraph's end, Franklin is more realistic about what he can accomplish. B cannot be correct because self-aggrandizement entails an exaggeratedly positive view of self; if one recognizes one's flaws, self-aggrandizement is not possible. Though it could be argued that in attempting moral perfection

Franklin has an overly developed sense of his capabilities, the end of the paragraph does not entail self-deprecation. Instead, Franklin merely points out the difficulties he has with his pursuit and thus develops a method to combat the difficulties he is encountering. He becomes realistic about what may or may not be possible: again, answer C. D is incorrect because although Franklin engages in self-assessment, he does not celebrate at the paragraph's end. Instead he recognizes how difficult is the task he has chosen to undertake. E sounds good and, in part, could also be correct. Franklin is ingenuous—he is direct and honest; however, there is no intuition involved at the paragraph's end, nor is Franklin's analysis of himself intuitive. It is empirical, because it is based on what he has experienced having undertaken the pursuit of moral perfection.

30. **C.** Franklin states that the "acquisition of some may facilitate the acquisition of certain others" (ll. 20–21). If you understand the sentence then you can easily discount the other answers. B and E might be attractive choices; however, if you have chosen either of these answers, you have not considered the sentence in its entirety. Franklin discusses the arrangement of his virtues; however, he states that he arranges them in a certain order precisely because the mastery of one virtue will "facilitate" mastery of the next. Answer A can be dismissed at first read because Franklin does not say that virtue attainment is an easy process, nor does he mention the importance of focus.

31. **E.** There are two analogies in this passage. The gardener and his beds is the first; the axe owner and the smith is the second. In order to choose the correct answer, close reading skills are required. In employing an analogy, Franklin is not discussing a real-life gardener and his beds. Moving through the analogy, the first point Franklin makes is that a gardener does not attempt to eradicate (eliminate or remove) all bad herbs in all beds at once (ll. 32–33). Thus, A can be eliminated. B relates to A because moving through one bed at a time is systematic. Franklin supports his systematic approach by stating that eradication of all the bad herbs at once would "exceed his reach and strength" (l. 33). Thus,

C can be eliminated because Franklin is constrained by what he believes is possible. *Constrain* means to limit or to restrict. D can be eliminated because the gardener does not move onto the next bed until he has accomplished his task of bad herb removal in the preceding bed (l. 34).

32. **D.** No mention is made of the need for a method for achieving the virtue of order, but here again, close reading is required. Franklin states, "a master… [must] often receive people of business at their own hours" (ll. 43–44). Thus, A can be eliminated. In line 47, Franklin says he has an "exceeding good memory." The implication of these words is that Franklin does not need order because he can remember where he has put things. B can therefore be eliminated. Franklin also claims that he "had not been early accustomed to it [order]" (l. 46). This implies that Franklin had either not been raised to be orderly or that he did not experience order in his youth. Regardless of which interpretation is most accurate, the point is that without growing up with order, order is difficult to establish as an adult—answer C. Understanding why E is true requires knowing what "sensible" (l. 47) means in context. Franklin's point is that he is not even aware of (not sensible of) not having order in his life; thus, he is unmotivated to achieve order.

33. **D.** As indicated in the above explanation, "sensible" means aware. Awareness is consciousness. Franklin is not "conscious" of a need for order.

34. **B.** Franklin claims, "I was not so sensible of the inconvenience attending want of method" (ll. 47–48). Here, Franklin's point is that he was not conscious of any inconvenience even if he lacked the method to attain order. Why is this? Because as he indicates earlier (see question 5), he has a good memory and was not trained to be orderly or to need order when he was young. In this context, "want" means lack; it does not mean to desire.

35. **C.** For this question, the attractive distracter is B. Franklin's desire for the virtue of order is thwarted. So, in order to choose C, you must

be able to understand the difference between resigned and accepting, as well as to correctly perceive Franklin's attitude. "Resigned" implies giving in reluctantly. Accepting, however, implies the recognition that something is true and tolerating it without protest or an attempt to change it. Looking at the end of the paragraph, Franklin states that like others who have tried to break bad habits, he has "given up the struggle and concluded that 'a speckled axe was best'" (ll. 63–64). Franklin's conclusion that the speckled axe is best indicates that he has accepted his inability to become morally perfect and no longer desires to change his behavior. Answer A might seem attractive; "vexed" (l. 49) can connote anger or irritation, but "annoyance" is closer to the true meaning of *vexed*. There is no hopefulness expressed in the paragraph. E might seem like a possibility, but "good-hearted" doesn't really describe Franklin's attitude as well as does C or even B. D can be eliminated at first read, as Franklin is not self-critical; he explains that order has been difficult to achieve because he hasn't minded not having order in his life. No criticism here. *Disdainful* means showing feelings of contempt or disrespect for something or somebody. Franklin embraces his inability to achieve order and moral perfection: thus, there is no contempt or disrespect implied.

36. **D**. For this question, knowledge of vocabulary is again crucial. If you do not know what *concede* and *enumerate* mean, you will have difficulty choosing the correct answer. *Concede* implies the acceptance of defeat. The man with the axe does not claim defeat; he states, "I like a speckled axe best" (l. 60). This is not a concession but a choice to keep the axe as it is, or in other words, to accept moral imperfections. A is therefore incorrect. *Enumerate* (answer E) means to name things on a list. There is no enumeration in the analogy. *Rationalize* implies justification, but in terms of what could be considered irrational or unacceptable behavior. Not seeking moral perfection is not irrational or unacceptable. In fact, it is not a goal for most of us! However, in accepting the axe, speckles and all, Franklin is justifying his decision. To justify implies inventing an excuse. It is reasonable not to continue with what seems not

worthwhile. That is why the man stops helping to have his axe ground, and that is why Franklin ceases striving for moral perfection (Answer D). C is obviously wrong because just as the man stops grinding his axe, Franklin ceases the attainment of moral perfection.

37. **B.** In order to answer this question correctly, you need to look at the conversation between the smith and the man with the axe. When the man with the axe wants to take his axe "as it was" (l. 58), the smith replies, "Turn on, turn on; we shall have it bright by-and-by; as yet it is only speckled" (ll. 59–60). The words of the smith imply that with continued hard work, the axe will be made bright. Thus, B is correct. The smith is helping the man by grinding the axe; however, this makes the man's job extremely difficult (ll. 54–56). Thus, answer A cannot be correct. C is incorrect because the smith's positive attitude does not affect the man's feelings of fatigue (ll. 55–56). Though the smith is encouraging, the man quits turning the wheel; thus, D is incorrect. E is incorrect because the answer has nothing to do with the relationship between the smith and the man. Further, the flaws do not make the axe valuable, and the axe's value is not even an issue in the analogy or what follows it.

38. **D.** The noun form of *countenance* means "face or facial expression." Thus A can be an attractive distracter. However, in this case, the word is used as a verb. *To countenance* means to approve, tolerate or accept. Franklin's point is that the possession of a few faults will help him keep his friends' approval because they need not envy or dislike him because of moral perfection. In fact, he implies that a truly kind man—a *benevolent* man—will ensure he is flawed for precisely this reason.

39. **D.** Close reading and vocabulary knowledge needed! D looks attractive as a choice because Franklin uses the word "reason" in line 65. However, what does he mean by this? Moral perfection seems like a worthy pursuit, a "reason" to go to "extreams" (l. 66), but in the end is most probably a "kind of foppery." A fop is a man who is so vain about his appearance that he is mocked by others. Franklin is saying that others

might ridicule his apparent self-absorption or vanity due to his pursuit of moral perfection. Therefore, A and E are also reasons not to pursue moral perfection. Moral perfection could, according to Franklin, be a misguided pursuit. C is also a reason to cease striving for moral perfection because, as lines 69–70 indicate, flaws help retain friends.

Passage 4

40. **B.** The author states in the first sentence of the excerpt that he wants to ensure that "the ties of brotherhood may still bind together the rich and the poor…." (l. 2). The use of the word "still" implies that the rich and the poor have had a bond of brotherhood in the past. This is an assumption, as he provides no evidence that such a bond has existed. Answer A is incorrect because the author's visit to the Sioux has not revealed anything about economic differences. Answer C is incorrect because it is from his visit to the Sioux that he concludes there is no difference between how the chief lives and how the tribe lives (ll. 4–6). His conclusion is based on empirical evidence. Answer D is incorrect because no one could argue with the fact that there are differences between how the rich and the poor live. Finally, Answer E is also incorrect because it is directly stated that over the past few hundred years, the conditions of human life have changed.

41. **A.** A catalogue is another word for a list. Lines 4–6 catalogue the various aspects of the lives of the Sioux to emphasize the fact that there was no difference in any aspects of their lives regardless of the position held. If you know the definition of the other devices and can recognize them in context, you can eliminate them, as they do not appear in the paragraph.

42. **D.** The author is comparing the lives of contemporary Indians to the lives of people who lived three hundred years earlier. His comparison implies a judgment. He judges the lives of the Indians as less civilized then the lives their contemporaries. You might find answer E attractive

as this comment is certainly dubious; however, the comment is not a testimonial. The author is not reporting on the qualities or virtues of the Indians. Answer A can be eliminated because it is certainly not obvious that the Indians are three hundred years behind their contemporaries. Answer C can be eliminated because the author's view of Indians does not reveal his views of civilization.

43. **D.** In order to answer this question correctly, you have to be able to understand the organization of the paragraph as a whole. The author's argument is that the "conditions of human life have not only been changed, but revolutionized, within the past few hundred years" (ll. 3–4). The author then goes on to claim that in the past there were no external differences between the lives of the poor and the rich. The discussion of the Sioux supports this claim. The last sentence of the paragraph is the evidence that supports his argument that today human conditions have changed. The contrast between the "palace of the millionaire" and the cottage of the laborer" (ll. 10–11) is evidence of this claim.

44. **B.** To answer this question, find the pronoun's antecedent—the noun to which the pronoun refers. "Change" appears twice in Paragraph 1, first in line 4 and then in line 12. Line 12 does not indicate to what "change" refers, so you must follow the trail back to line 3, where the change is defined: "the conditions of human life have not only been changed, but revolutionized...." Once you have followed the pronoun trail, you can eliminate the other answers.

45. **D.** The author's comment as cited in the stem asserts that either there are people with wealth who recognize and possess what is "highest and best in the arts" (ll. 15–16) or there is "universal squalor" (l. 18). The author's point rests on the idea that without inequality, everyone would be poor. It should be obvious that this either/or reasoning is false. It ignores the possibility that all people could become wealthy. The other rhetorical fallacies listed in the answer choices are discussed in the rhetoric section of the book.

46. **A.** In order to answer this question, you must refer to the footnote. As the author has preceded this reference with what I have discussed in the answer to question 7, it should be evident that the only point about Maecenas that is important is that he was a patron of the arts. Answer D might seem attractive, but it is only an aspect of the answer. Aspects are not correct; don't choose them. "Arts" is the category into which poetry falls.

47. **B.** To answer this question correctly, consider both paragraphs 1 and 2. The key argument the author makes is that the conditions of human life have been revolutionized. Paragraph 2 explains why this change "is not to be deplored, but welcomed as highly beneficial" (ll. 13–14). Though whom this change benefits, and how it does so, may be arguable, it is nonetheless true that the author provides justification for the argument with which the excerpt begins. Answer A might seem attractive; however, there are no assumptions in paragraph 1 apart from the implied assumption about the state of Indian life. Answers C and D can be eliminated because the author feels no need to defend his views on class differences and there is no discussion of his political views. Answer E can be easily eliminated because E is only an aspect of what is included in paragraph 2.

48. **D.** This question requires that you be familiar with rhetorical appeals, rhetorical devices, and rhetorical fallacies. Faulty causality is the establishment of a cause-and-effect relationship when none exists. A second event can follow a first, but the first does not necessarily cause the second. In paragraph 3 the author discusses the history of the manufacture of products, with a particular focus on the master/apprentice relationship. Paragraph 4 begins with the claim that "such a mode of manufacture was crude articles at high prices" (l. 39–40). The author views the master/apprentice relationship and the way goods were manufactured as the cause of unskilled goods sold at exorbitant prices. It is difficult to believe that nothing beautiful, useful or artistic was produced during this period. Thus, the cause and effect created by the author is illogical. An appeal to logos is an appeal to reason. It is reflected in an

author's use of reason and rational ideas such as the use of credible evidence like facts and statistics, though even facts and statistics can be manipulated. No such usage exists in the first sentence of paragraph 4. An appeal to tradition is the claim that because something has historically been done one way, it should continue to be done in that way. This, too, does not exist in the cited sentence. Answer E is incorrect because no extended comparison exists. Answer A can easily be eliminated because the sentence contains no contradiction. Appeals and logical fallacies are discussed in the section on rhetoric. If you need a more thorough explanation, refer to this section.

49. **A.** This question requires that you read each answer choice carefully and see which ones appear in the paragraph. Answer B is implied in lines 43–44: "the poor enjoy what the rich could not before afford." Answers C and D are indicated in lines 47–48: "The landlord has books...than the king could obtain." Answer D is revealed in lines 43–44: "What were luxuries have become the necessity of life." Answer A is incorrect because the author states nothing about the happiness of people today.

50. **D.** *Salutary* means "beneficial." Answers B and E might seem attractive, but the results of the change that the author describes in Paragraph 4 are neither useful nor required. The purchase of luxuries is not necessarily useful, and the purchase of commodities at low prices is not necessarily a requirement. Think of your own recent purchases and the luxuries you have in your own homes. The change is not doubtful; it is factual. It is also not misguided, because according to the author, all benefit.

51. **C.** Context provides the clue to meaning. The clue to the answer lies in what precedes it. "We assemble thousands of operatives in the factory...*of whom the employer can know little or nothing*" (ll. 49–51). If the employer cannot know her or his employees, it can be assumed that the same is true of the employees. Thus, the use of the word "myth" implies that the employer is not present. None of the other meanings fit the context in which the word is used.

52. **E.** Ask yourself why the "employer is forced into the strictest economies." The answer is, for no other reason than "law of competition" (ll. 56). The word "among" follows the phrase cited in the stem. "Among" is a preposition indicating something or somebody in a group. Here "among" refers to the results of being forced into the "strictest economies." None of the other answers choices answer the question why.

Section II

Essay 1: Responses

Response 1

In the past, libraries, managed by librarians, were places where information was housed and accessed in the form of books and other print media. With the advent of technology and online resources, libraries are being forced to change. Librarians are now called information specialists because information no longer exists only on the page in a book, newspaper or periodical. However, the fact that information can be easily accessed via the Internet does not mean that the books in libraries are obsolete. Though libraries need to consider how to optimize their space for digital and Web-based research, they also need to ensure that their book and print sources not only remain intact but also continue to grow.

Currently, libraries do an excellent job of meeting the needs of a variety of people for both print and Web materials. Source A lists all of the many services the Chicago Public Libraries provide. Further, this source points out, "Last year, Chicagoans checked out nearly 10 million items from the Chicago Public Library's 74 locations and the majority of those items were books...." Even in the 21st century, people like to read books for pleasure. Libraries are one of the few places where a book can be read for free. Because new books are being published all the time, libraries need to continue to purchase books so that those who want to read books for free can.

Anyone who does research needs access to books. Source E discusses the specific information needs of "scholars" as opposed to "information seekers." Scholars "wish to find *current* books on a subject categorized with the *prior* books on the same subject, so that the newer works can be perceived in the context of the existing literature…" (Source E). One way libraries catalogue and organize their books is under subject headings. This type of organization allows people to read about their subject in a variety of sources from differing time periods. The comprehensive context encountered on the shelves of libraries is a result of the expertise of librarians. It is they who have been trained to decide what is important and what is significant. This is an advantage to researchers who then do not have to engage in the initial sifting process required by Internet research.

In the cartoon provided in Source F, a woman is talking to a young boy in a library. She states, "It's a library, honey—kind of an earlier version of the World Wide Web." The idea is that the younger generation uses the Internet so much that they do not even know what a library is. The cartoon reveals what many would argue, that libraries, with their many stacks of countless books, are overwhelming, confusing and intimidating. Further, few would refute the claim that kids growing up today do not go to libraries as frequently as they once did for information or fun; instead, they go to their computers. However, as Source D points out, "If students aren't checking out books, or aren't getting unrestricted, immediate access to books, they are missing out on a vital source of instruction…as a medium for both storing and dispensing information, books rival, even surpass, their digital counterparts" (Source D). There is no denying that the Internet is an easy and useful tool that meets many needs. Though it might be too far to go to state that books surpass their digital counterparts, Source D's claim that books remain essential should not be dismissed. Therefore, though libraries must embrace the changes wrought by the technological revolution, they should not sacrifice their book collections to do so. Books remain necessary for education, information, and pleasure.

Libraries face difficult times. States and universities are cutting their funding to them. However, what Source F claims about Harvard is true for our society. "The greatness of this [society] … in the future rests on the greatness of our librar[ies]." At one time, the primary function of libraries was to select and organize the best, most important and cutting-edge books on a wide range of topics so that the public could have access to them. This primary function is as relevant today as it was in the past. The Internet simply cannot offer what is offered by the books in libraries.

Response 2

I grew up in a small town going to the library every week with my sisters and my mother. We would spend a few hours there every Saturday morning carefully choosing our books and talking to the librarians about our interests and the books that would meet them. I loved the quiet of the library and the smell of the books as they rested on their shelves. Times have changed from even when I was a little girl. Neither I nor my friends visit libraries that often. We use our computers for any research projects we are assigned and to interact socially. Also, I got a Kindle for Christmas, so I now use this to read books. I don't think libraries should eliminate their print and book sources completely, but I do think that space must be made for digital and Web-based research.

Cushing Academy in New England has removed all the books from its library. "When I look at books, I see an outdated technology, like scrolls before books,' said James Tracy, headmaster of Cushing (Source B). Tracy's view of books as "outdated technology" is true of the reality of my friends and me. We have yet to need a print book other than the books assigned to us to read for a class in school. I do not know if Cushing was correct to eliminate all of its books, but it is true that their library is "a model for the 21st-century school." The 21st century is about technology, and technology's importance will only continue as the century progresses.

The change Tracy made in Cushing's library is beginning to be mirrored in university libraries as well. "For the last ten years or so, books have been slowly phased out of a college student's life and personal computers have been phased in. Increasingly, materials are available online both on the Internet and through online journal databases" (Source C).

As I said earlier, physical books do not play much of a role in my own education. Libraries, aware of this trend, are rightly working to create spaces and provide access to resources that reflect this trend.

Some would argue that the importance of technology and its progress is overrated and that predictions about its role in the future inaccurate. Source D cites Scott Celsor, a doctoral candidate in theology at Marquette University. In response to the new library that is being built there that will house very few books, Celsor states, "It concerns me that they are overemphasizing the role of technology in the future" (Source D). Others echo the dean at Marquette who says that "prognosticators are not always accurately predicting" (Source D). Though it is true that the future role of technology remains unclear, technology is certainly is not going to be used any less than it is now. I know I could never break myself of the habit of finding answers to my questions by searching online. I also know that I could not give up Facebook or the convenience of my Kindle. Whether we like it or not, technology is here to stay and libraries must accept this reality if they are to remain relevant in the 21st century.

In the cartoon provided in source F, a woman about 50 or 60 years old is talking to a little boy. She states, "It's a library, honey—kind of an earlier version of the World Wide Web." In the front of the cartoon are two tall stacks of books. Behind the woman and the boy are even more stacks of books. The fact that the woman calls a library an "earlier version of the World Wide Web" is important. "Earlier" usually implies less advanced. In many ways, libraries are less advanced than the Web. The Web is a fast and easy way to access up-to-date information of all kind from all over the world. Finding information in the library is time-consuming and tedious, and the information can be dated. The cartoon points out that the young generation has evolved away from books. We go online for what we need and libraries must have the space and resources for us to do this or they will become places that we no longer visit.

I do not look forward to a future in which libraries are completely bookless and printless. However, libraries of the future must be places where people can access the resources that exist on the Internet. Though I have fond memories of the hours I spent in the library as a little girl finding and reading books, these are not necessarily the memories I would want for my own children. The world is changing as a result of technology. Libraries cannot ignore this change and continue to survive and flourish.

COMMENTARY

Score: 7 or 8

These two essays are included for two reasons. The first reason is to demonstrate that your response to the synthesis question can be personal—it can include references to yourself and your own experience. The second reason is to show that arguments in response to the prompt will differ. These two argue opposite points.

Before analyzing why and how these essays are effective, it is important to be able to identify whether these essays have challenged, defended, or qualified the claim in the prompt. Here is the prompt again:

> Read the following seven sources carefully, including the introductory information. Then synthesize information from at least three of the sources and incorporate it into a coherent, well-developed essay that defends, challenges, or qualifies the claim that in the digital age, it is appropriate for libraries to shrink or eliminate their book and print sources in an effort to optimize their space for digital and Web-based research.

Here are the thesis statements:

> **Response 1:** Though libraries need to consider how to optimize their space for digital and Web-based research, they also need to ensure that their book and print sources not only remain intact but also continue to grow.

> **Response 2:** I don't think libraries should eliminate their print and book sources completely, but I do think that space must be made for digital and Web-based research.

Take a moment to consider what the thesis statements are arguing. Notice that each thesis *qualifies* the claim in the prompt. Response 1 recognizes that "space is needed for digital and Web-based research" BUT argues that "libraries need to ensure that their book and print sources not only remain intact but also continue to grow." Response 2 recognizes that libraries should not eliminate their print and book sources *completely* BUT argues that "space must be made for digital and Web-based research." Qualifying means that you explore both sides of the claim but argue one side more.

What Each Response Does Well

Each response begins with a valid introduction that leads nicely into the thesis. Response 1 begins with a discussion of the roles of libraries and moves to why libraries must continue to maintain their print and book sources. Response 2 begins with a personal anecdote and again, moves smoothly into why libraries must change as a result of technological advances. Each type of introduction is valid.

Each response does a good job of employing quotations to support the thesis statements. The supporting paragraphs have topic sentences that are then followed by quotations from the sources that are relevant to the topic of the paragraph as previewed in the topic sentence. The quotations are led into well—no dumping here. Each quotation is then followed by an explanation and an argument in support of the thesis. Here is a paragraph from Response 1. The parentheses that precede the sentences indicate what is occurring.

[Topic sentence] Currently, libraries do an excellent job of meeting the needs of a variety of people for both print and web materials. [background and lead into quotation] Source A lists all of the many services the Chicago Public Libraries provide. Further, this source points out that [quotation from source] "Last year, Chicagoans checked out nearly 10 million items from the Chicago Public Library's 74 locations and the majority of those items were books…" (Source A). [engagement of quotation in the service of the essay's argument] Even in the 21st century, people like to read books for pleasure. Libraries are the only places where an actual book can be read for free. **[final argument in support of thesis]** Because new books are being published all the time, libraries need to continue to purchase books so that those who want to read books free can.

Moving on to the visual-analysis paragraphs, what is important to note is how each essay uses the visual. After describing the cartoon, Response 1 uses the visual as a concession: "The cartoon reveals what many would argue, that libraries, with their many stacks of countless books are overwhelming, confusing, and intimidating. Further, few would refute the claim that kids growing up today rarely go to libraries for information or fun; instead, they go to their computers." If you remember, concessions must be refuted or your thesis will be undermined. Response 1 signals the beginning of the refutation with a "however." "However, as source D points out, 'If students aren't checking out books, or aren't getting unrestricted, immediate access to books, they are missing out on a vital source of instruction...as a medium for both storing and dispensing information, books rival, even surpass, their digital counterparts' (Source D)." The argument of the refutation is then continued and completed. "There is no denying that the Internet is an easy and useful tool that meets many needs. Though it might be too far to go to state that books surpass their digital counterparts, Source D's claim that books remain essential should not be dismissed. Therefore, though libraries must embrace the changes wrought by the technological revolution, they should not sacrifice their book collections to do so. Books remain necessary for education, information and pleasure."

Response 2 uses the cartoon in support of the argument made in the thesis. "The fact that the woman calls a library an 'earlier version of the World Wide Web' is important. 'Earlier' usually implies less advanced. In many ways, libraries are less advanced than the Web. The Web is a fast and easy way to access up-to-date information of all kind from all over the world. Finding information in the library is time-consuming and tedious, and the information can be dated." The final argument for the thesis is "The cartoon points out that the young generation has evolved away from books. We go online for what we need, and libraries must have the space and resources for us to do this or they will become places that we no longer visit."

In the fourth paragraph of response 2, the author strengthens the argument by making a concession to an alternative viewpoint, then refuting it.

- **Concession:** "Some would argue that the importance of technology and its progress is overrated and that predictions about its role in the future are inaccurate. Source D cites Scott Celsor, a doctoral candidate in theology at Marquette University. In response to the new library that is being built there that will house very few books, Celsor states, 'It concerns me that they are overemphasizing the role of technology in the future' (Source D). Others echo the dean at Marquette who says that 'prognosticators are not always accurately predicting' (Source D)."

- **Refutation:** "Though it is true that the future role of technology remains unclear, technology is certainly not going to be used any less than it is now. I know I could never break myself of the habit of finding answers to my questions by searching online. I also know that I could not give up Facebook or the convenience of my Kindle. Whether we like it or not, technology is here to stay and libraries must accept this reality if they are to remain relevant in the 21st century."

You may not have the time to write a conclusion as complete as the ones in the above responses. Even if this is the case, it is important to note why each conclusion is successful. Response 1 begins by repeating some of what is stated in the introduction to the assignment. "Libraries face difficult times. States and universities are cutting their funding to them." This works because the conclusion uses this only as a jumping-off point for the author's own ideas. Though the author cites a source, the words of the source are changed slightly to reflect the author's conclusion.

"However, what Source F claims about Harvard is true for our society. 'The greatness of this [society] … in the future rests on the greatness of our librar[ies].' At one time, the primary function of libraries was to select and organize the best, most important and cutting-edge books on a wide range of topics so that the public could have access to them. This primary function is as relevant today as it was in the past. The Internet simply cannot offer what is offered by the books in libraries."

The conclusion to Response 2 is personal, in keeping with the personal tone of the essay. "I do not look forward to a future in which libraries are completely bookless and printless. However, libraries of the future must be places where people can access the resources that exist on the Internet. Though I have fond memories of the hours I spent in the library as a little girl finding and reading books, these are not necessarily the memories I would want for my own children. The world is changing as a result of technology. Libraries cannot ignore this change and continue to survive and flourish."

Each conclusion begins with the topic of the essay written but then moves on to make a final, new and original point. These conclusions conclude; they do not summarize. Finally, neither response merely summarizes or paraphrases the sources provided. Instead, they both use the sources to support the argument stated in the thesis. Merely summarizing or paraphrasing the sources will earn you a low score.

Essay 2: Responses

Response 1

Throughout history, African American people have experienced prejudice and slavery. They are not able to lead the same lives as white people. This can be very difficult for them. Being a black male is even harder. They create fear in people. In the excerpt from his essay, Brent Staples makes clear that he experiences racial profiling: white people assume that since Staples is a black male, he is dangerous.

Staples opens his essay with an ironic comment. "My first victim was a woman—white, well-dressed, in her late twenties" (l. 1). This woman is not a "victim" in any sense of the word. Staples neither threatens nor harms her. The only thing this woman is a victim of is Staples' presence, which he describes from her perspective as "menacingly close" (ll. 8–9). A "menace" evokes images of a gangster or hoodlum that is dangerous. It is Staple's proximity that distresses her even though he has done nothing to elicit this distress. She runs from him. This incident reveals that regardless of the intentions of an African American male, his mere presence in public, late at night, creates fear.

Years later Staples recalls the incident when the woman ran from him. "It was clear that she thought herself the quarry of a mugger…or worse. Suffering a bout of insomnia, however, I was stalking sleep, not defenseless wayfarers" (ll. 16–18). Here, Staples personifies sleep. "Sleep" is not a person or an animal. It therefore cannot be stalked. Staples plays on the connotation of "stalk" to make his point that as a result of insomnia, it was sleep he desired, not a victim on whom to perpetrate a crime.

The reaction of the white public, particularly women, continues to affect Staples. He feels like "an accomplice in tyranny" (l. 17). A tyrant is a cruel and unjust ruler. As the "tyrant's accomplice," Staples feels that it is him, not her reaction, that is the problem. Staples goes on to point out that this feeling does not go away. It is confirmed by other such encounters. "That first encounter, and those that followed, signified that a vast, unnerving gulf lay between nighttime pedestrians—particularly women—and me" (ll. 19–21). "Unnerving gulf" underscores Staples' point about feeling like a tyrant's henchman. A "gulf" can signify a distance that is unbreachable. Staples does not enjoy this gulf; he is "unnerved" by it because people react to his skin color, not to who he really is. His use of onomatopoeia when he states every time he crossed the street he heard the "thunk, thunk, thunk of the driver…hammering down the door locks" (l. 28) hammers home his point. White people respond to him with fear because he is a black male.

Staples understands why, particularly at night, women respond to him by clutching their purses and increasing their pace. They have reason to be afraid because they are vulnerable. "Yet these truths are no solace against the kind of alienation that comes of being ever the suspect, a fearsome entity with whom pedestrians avoid making eye contact… (ll. 45–46). Staples juxtaposes his feelings of "alienation" to "fearsome entity" to reveal that being forever and always feared makes him feel estranged from humanity. Racial profiling, though he concedes that there are reasons for this profiling, has made him feel disconnected from his fellow human beings.

Staples describes his "ability to alter public space" as "ugly" (l. 13). He does not enjoy the reactions he elicits in others on the streets of New York or any city for that matter. He has to "smother his rage" (l. 52). It's too bad that we do not live in a colorblind society. If we did, white people would not flee from the presence of African American men like Staples, nor would Staples have to fear that someone will misread his reactions and mistakenly shoot at him, causing his injury or death.

Response 2

We live in a society full of hatred and prejudice. This applies to black people too. White people fear black people and black males are even scarier. Brent Staples uses specific word choice to convey his view about what it means to be an African American male in society today.

In paragraph one, Staples states. "My first victim was a woman—white, well-dressed in her late twenties" (l. 1). Staples uses the word "victim" to describe the woman, but she is not a "victim." She runs from Staples because she is afraid. Her fear victimizes her.

Being an African American man can be dangerous. "And I soon gathered that being perceived as dangerous is a hazard in itself. I only needed to turn a corner into a dicey situation, or crowd some frightened, armed person in a foyer somewhere, or make an errant move after being pulled over by a policeman" (ll. 25–29). Staples catalogues all the bad things that can happen to him because he is black even though he is innocent. It's not easy being a black man. He could get killed even if he didn't do anything.

Staples catalogues the people he has problems with because of the color of his skin. "Then there were the standard unpleasantries with policemen, doormen, bouncers, cabdrivers, and others whose business it is to screen out troublesome individuals before there is any nastiness" (ll. 37–40). People assume that he will cause trouble, but he wouldn't.

In order to make sure that people don't fear him when he is out late, Staples whistles classical music. I guess we live in a society that assumes if you know classical music you cannot be a mugger. We need to work together to overcome prejudice.

COMMENTARY

Response 1

Score: 7

This is a fairly strong essay. The thesis is accurate and supported well by rhetorical analysis and argument. The introduction, however, is weakened by a generalization about prejudice against black people. This adds little to the essay. The introduction makes a point about black people not being able "to lead the same lives as white people" and how black males create fear. Neither of these comments is fully explained. Thus, the introduction is neither as clear nor as accurate as it could be. This stops the essay from scoring a 9. The essay is organized by idea, not by rhetorical device, which strengthens the essay.

Each topic is supported by a quotation. Each quotation is analyzed, and then an argument is formed that links paragraph to thesis. High marks for this. Paragraph 3 is particularly impressive because it brings together three separate quotations that all relate to the topic of the paragraph. This paragraph ends with a play on Staples' own word "hammer," exhibiting a sophisticated use of language. In paragraph 5, the essay takes note of Staples' concession and refutation. This is a sophisticated move. The conclusion makes good use of a quotation from Staples about "public space" and his ability to "alter it.' However, the conclusion, like the introduction, includes a superficial and somewhat meaningless point about the desire for a "colorblind society." If this had been left out, the conclusion would have been more powerful and might have lifted the essay up to level of an 8 or a 9.

Response 2

Score: 3

The first paragraph is disjointed and unclear. The points are discon-nected and random. The thesis is a statement of the obvious—of course Staples uses word choice. Without words, there would be no excerpt. Another problem is that the essay does not stick to its thesis. "Word choice" is the rhetorical device and yet the essay analyzes cataloguing. Thus, paragraphs 2 and 3 are off topic. The essay refers to "paragraph one." It is best never to refer to the passage as a passage in this way. For example, you would not want to write, "in line 22 Staples claims." In the conclusion, the employment of "you" serves only to weaken an already weak paragraph. "We need to work together to overcome prejudice" is not a compelling call to action but rather a statement of the obvious.

Final Note: There are many ways to approach rhetorical analysis. You might find a device that you feel is worthy of analysis, while another person may focus on another strategy. Variety in responses is expected. What matters is how well you analyze and make an argument.

Essay 3: Responses

Response 1

Erich Fromm's assertion that "the capacity to doubt" may be all that saves human civilization may seem extreme, but given the historical context in which he made this statement, his belief is understandable. Blind obedience to an authority that demands an individual "turn his key" and unleash nuclear weapons could in fact result in an end to civi-lization. Given the dangers in the world from fundamentalist terrorism, nuclear proliferation, and unthinking acceptance of dogma, the presence of doubt, criticism, and disobedience might just be humankind's sole salvation.

It is important to note that Fromm is probably not advocating dis-obedience for disobedience's sake. Just doing the opposite of what an authority figure instructs is not disobedience; it is contrariness. Fromm's phrase "the capacity to disobey" suggests that there may be many times when obedience is appropriate or preferable. In some situations, rules are intended to preserve the safety of individuals. Blatantly disregarding the prohibition against drunk driving, for example, just because the government tells us it isn't safe to drive while intoxicated, is not a case of critical thinking or thoughtful disobedience. This is an example of an irresponsible act of disobedience. It lacks the moral strength of the Freedom Riders' civil disobedience in the 1960s, or of anti-war protesters who passively allow themselves to be jailed for their political beliefs. Some laws require blind obedience—they have been carefully reviewed and voted upon by legitimately elected government officials, approved by a democratically elected president, and vetted by our nation's judicial branch, the Supreme Court.

In other situations, however, it is more appropriate to follow Fromm's advice. The order in which he lists the necessary steps of disobedience—"doubt," "criticize," "disobey"—is instructive. First, it is vital to be skeptical of authority. What is the hidden agenda at work in the establishing of laws, rules, or orders? Who stands to profit from these rules? What will the consequences of obedience be? Questioning what lies behind an authority figure's edicts is healthy and reveals an intelligent mind at work. Criticism, Fromm's second action, is a move beyond doubt and suggests an active engagement with the pros and cons of obedience and disobedience. Criticism implies positing alternate routes of action, not just berating an authority figure. It is a constructive process. Disobedience is a last resort, and Fromm puts it last in his statement. Disobedience comes after reflection and critical engagement with a moral quandary. It is not a knee-jerk reaction to an unconsidered situation. For Fromm, writing at the time of the Cuban missile crisis, disobedience could have meant the difference between life and death, as Kennedy and Kruschev faced each other eye to eye, armed with nuclear weapons. Each man had to do what he thought was right and required, but Kruschev's "blink"—which could be construed as an act of disobedience against those in his government who advocated nuclear war—might have saved the fate of the entire world.

An awareness of what we are obeying and whether or not we are justified in our obedience is all that Fromm calls for. Our "capacity" to disobey, not blind disobedience itself, is what Fromm's words seem to emphasize. Having the potential to disobey an order implies that we are capable, that we are mature individuals who can judge rules, regulations, and orders responsibly based on their own merits. If we unthinkingly rely on authority figures to make decisions for us we will not be acting in authentic, individual ways that could promote morals, safety, and progress.

Response 2

Erich Fromm regards the capacity to disobey as important for human survival. Such a statement is bold and even shocking, but it raises the question, "What is so good about disobeying authority?" After all, we are taught from an early age to obey our parents, listen to our teachers, do what our bosses tell us to do, pay our taxes on time, and follow the rules that our elected officials set. It might be important to think for ourselves sometimes, but Fromm puts too much emphasis on the value of disobedience. Doing what we are told is necessary for the smooth and continued functioning of civilization.

Evaluating situations is critical for survival. It is a good thing to criticize the way things have been done in the past to see if they were really done the best way. In this area, Fromm is correct. If a teacher always teaches the way he has been taught and doesn't take into consideration changing technology, differences in students' abilities, or current events, then that teacher is probably not going to be effective. Teachers who constantly expect students to fill out boring note cards for their research papers when most students are working with cut and paste documents from the Internet ask students to do unnecessary work that just wastes time and isn't helpful. It is better when teachers ask the question, "Why are we doing this task in this way?" and then make changes to the research process to help their students learn more effectively.

In other areas, though, challenging authority is a bad idea, and in some situations, it might even be dangerous to do so. Imagine an army in which every soldier could question his superior officers' orders, or if the best way to attack the enemy was voted on and decided by a simple majority. It would be crazy, and people would be getting killed all the time. Or what about a high school where the majority—the students—got to decide what the graduation requirements should be or how teachers got to teach? Many of my friends would not even go to school at such a place. In these examples, it is important to obey one's "superiors," those people who have more experience and knowledge and authority and who can make educated decisions on behalf of the masses.

Rather than losing "the capacity to disobey," as Fromm puts it, people should disobey only when the authority they are disobeying is clearly wrong or immoral. Most of the time, it makes more sense to defer to others who know more. It might be that if you do this, then you will eventually learn the things you need to know in order to be an authority, and then other people will have to listen to you and you can make good decisions, decisions that might someday "stand between a future for mankind and an end to civilization."

COMMENTARY

Response 1

Score: 8

This is an effective essay. The introduction is specific and focused. The thesis is well written and clear. The second paragraph clarifies the thesis and the author's take on Fromm's claim by explaining "Fromm is probably not advocating disobedience for disobedience's sake." This topic is developed convincingly through examples. The essay draws an interesting contrast between "an irresponsible act of disobedience" and one that has "moral strength" like "the Freedom Riders' civil disobedience in the 1960s, or of anti-war protesters who passively allow themselves to be jailed for their political beliefs." The transition sentence at the opening of Paragraph 3 is effective. (As an aside, transitions are not required. It is better to leave them out than to use them poorly.) This essay, too, employs rhetorical questions; however, here the questions are examples of what should be asked of authority before one agrees to obey. Thus, they are useful and add meaning, unlike the rhetorical question in Response 1. In this paragraph, the author of the essay makes an interesting point about Fromm's statement: "The order in which he lists the necessary steps of disobedience—'doubt,' 'criticize,' 'disobey'—is instructive." This paragraph includes a unique take on Fromm's claim, and the essay takes this point further by interpreting Fromm's words. The conclusion makes an excellent point that begins with Fromm's point yet moves beyond what the essay has already argued. "Having the potential to disobey an order implies that we are capable, that we are mature individuals who can judge rules, regulations, and orders responsibly based on their own merits. If we unthinkingly rely on authority figures to make decisions for us we will not be acting in authentic, individual ways that could promote morals, safety, and progress." What keeps this essay from scoring a 9 is that one more paragraph is needed to develop the claim in the thesis. Paragraph 2, though useful, explicates how the author of the essay interprets Fromm's idea of disobedience instead of providing support for the author's thesis. The essay is well written. The syntax and diction choices are accurate and sophisticated. The author of the essay has also done a nice job of showcasing his or her knowledge of the world at large. This knowledge is impressive and impressively incorporated into the essay's argument.

Response 2

Score: 3

This essay fails to respond adequately to the prompt. Though the introduction is fairly sound, it suffers from the meaningless rhetorical question problem, thereby wasting the reader's time. This, in and of itself, would not hurt the essay's score, but the essay has other flaws. Though the thesis is clear and would have made for an interesting persuasive essay, it is not supported by what follows in the body of the essay. If we apply the "one reason my thesis is true because" rule, it should be clear that what paragraph 2 begins with—"Evaluating situations is critical for survival"—is not a reason in support of the thesis "Doing what we are told is necessary for the smooth and continued functioning of civilization." "Evaluating situations" has nothing to do with the necessity for obedience. Paragraph 3 is more effective than paragraph 2 in that the topic sentence is a reason that can support the thesis. However, the evidence provided in this paragraph is unconvincing and in some cases, irrelevant. The second sentence begins well. "Imagine an army in which every soldier could question his superior officers' orders…" but unfortunately then veers off topic "if the best way to attack the enemy was voted on and decided by a simple majority." Voting, like evaluating, has nothing to do with obedience. The conclusion begins well and could have gone on to make an interesting point about disobeying an immoral authority. However, like much of the essay, it too veers off in a direction unrelated to the point with which the paragraph begins. The essay is clearly written and easy to follow. However, the use of over-long sentences and unsophisticated syntax structure ensures that the essay remain in the lower range of scores. The final sentence of the essay is four lines long. The length alone should have signaled to the writer that the sentence needed to be restructured. As elsewhere indicated, avoid "you"!

About the Author

Jocelyn Sisson has been teaching English for more than twenty years in both private and public schools. Sisson lives in Indianapolis, Indiana, and teaches at North Central High School, a diverse urban-suburban high school of 3,600 students. She teaches AP English Language and Composition and college-level composition classes. She also blogs on the current state of education for the *Indianapolis Star*. Sisson holds a BA from Brown University and a masters' degree from Harvard University.

Notes

Notes

Notes

Notes

Notes

Notes

Also Available

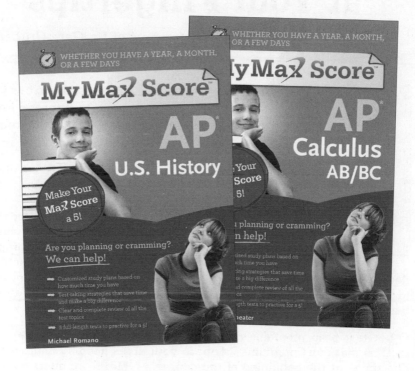

My Max Score AP U.S. History
by Michael Romano • 978-1-4022-4310-3

My Max Score AP English Literature and Composition
by Tony Armstrong • 978-1-4022-4311-0

My Max Score AP Calculus AB/BC
by Carolyn Wheater • 978-1-4022-4313-4

My Max Score AP U.S. Government & Politics
by Del Franz • 978-1-4022-4314-1

$14.99 U.S./ $17.99 CAN/ £9.99 UK

To download additional AP practice tests and learn more about My Max Score, visit mymaxscore.com.

Online Test Prep at Your Fingertips

Based on the Strategies and Refreshers of Dr. Gary Gruber.

Discover the areas you need to improve and learn proven strategies to maximize your score

MyMaxScore is a truly innovative program that will revolutionize how students prepare for standardized tests. It's simply the best SAT/ACT prep solution out there! Each student receives an individualized experience focusing specifically on areas in which he/she is weak and spends less time on areas that have already been mastered.

Other test prep programs claim to offer truly personalized prep. The truth is that most programs diagnose your areas needing improvement one time—at the beginning of the course. MyMaxScore offers so much more than that—it actually adapts to your strengths and weaknesses after EVERY practice question! The program continually monitors your progress and serves up questions only in the areas you need to improve.

Online SAT/ACT prep adapts to you continuously

- ✔ How you answer determines what you study
- ✔ Focus remains on improving unique weaknesses
- ✔ Reports your progress at every step in real time
- ✔ No driving to classes. No more wasted Saturdays.
- ✔ 30 minutes a day
- ✔ Increase confidence. Raise scores.

Sign up for a FREE Trial

Go to MyMaxScore.com today to learn more about how you can max your score!

Essentials from
Dr. Gary Gruber
and the creators of My Max Score

"Gruber can ring the bell on any number
of standardized exams."
—*Chicago Tribune*

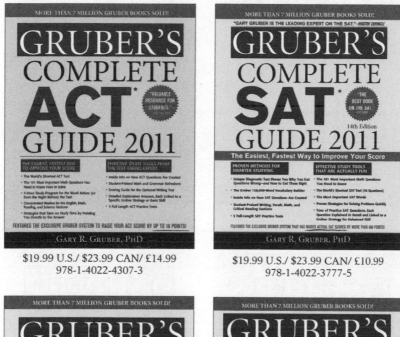

$19.99 U.S./ $23.99 CAN/ £14.99
978-1-4022-4307-3

$19.99 U.S./ $23.99 CAN/ £10.99
978-1-4022-3777-5

$16.99 U.S./ $19.99 CAN/ £11.99
978-1-4022-4308-0

$13.99 U.S./ $16.99 CAN/ £7.99
978-1-4022-3859-8

"Gruber's methods make the questions
seem amazingly simple to solve."
—*Library Journal*

"Gary Gruber is the leading expert on the SAT."
—*Houston Chronicle*

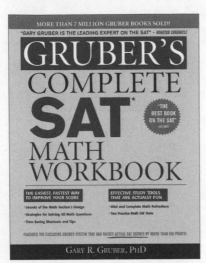

$14.99 U.S./ $15.99 CAN/ £7.99
978-1-4022-1846-0

$14.99 U.S./ $15.99 CAN/ £7.99
978-1-4022-1847-7

$14.99 U.S./ $15.99 CAN/ £7.99
978-1-4022-1848-4

$12.99 U.S./ $15.99 CAN/ £6.99
978-1-4022-2010-4